Bologna Mia

Bologna Mia

Memories from the Kitchen of Italy

Loretta Paganini

With Illustrations by **Doris Turner**

St Martin's Press

New York

THOMAS DUNNE BOOKS.
An imprint of St. Martin's Press.

BOLOGNA MIA: MEMORIES FROM THE KITCHEN OF ITALY. Copyright © 2000 by Loretta Paganini. All rights reserved. Printed in the United States of America. No part of this book may be used or reproduced in any manner whatsoever without written permission except in the case of brief quotations embodied in critical articles or reviews. For information, address St. Martin's Press, 175 Fifth Avenue, New York, N.Y. 10010.

www.stmartins.com

Design by Patrice Sheridan

LIBRARY OF CONGRESS CATALOGING-IN-PUBLICATION DATA
Paganini, Loretta.
    Bologna mia : memoirs from the kitchen of Italy / Loretta Paganini with
illustrations by Doris Turner. — 1st ed.
        p. cm.
    ISBN 0-312-26208-6
    1. Cookery, Italian. 2. Bologna (Italy) I. Title.
TX723 .P28 2000
641.5945'41—dc21

                                                                00-024272

First Edition: August 2000

Design by Patrice Sheridan

10   9   8   7   6   5   4   3   2   1

I dedicate this book

to my mother, Tilde, and my father, Elio,

for giving me life;

to my husband, Emil,

for teaching me how to enjoy life;

and to my daughters, Elizabeth, Stefanie, and

Julia,

for sharing with me the true meaning of life.

Contents

Contents

ix

Acknowledgments

First and most important, I want to thank my daughter Stefanie for writing this cookbook with me. Just as my mother shared her culinary knowledge with me, it was wonderful to be able to share our family history and my love for Italy with her. Even though she is by profession an attorney, I hope she continues the culinary tradition here in the United States with her family.

My husband, Emil, who loves me enough to tell me when something doesn't work, was my rock throughout this project. When I married and moved to the United States, I spoke no English. A special thank you to my mother-in-law, Myrtle, who took me by the hand, taught me about American life, and accepted me as one of her daughters.

I met Doris Turner right after I moved to our new home. She welcomed me into the neighborhood with a cherry pie made from the trees in her front yard. From that day on, Doris and her husband, Milton, have become a part of our family. I want to thank her for bringing my recipes and stories to life with her incredible illustrations. She also encouraged me to take classes at the Cordon Bleu in Paris as she had done and then to write this cookbook.

To my father, who walked with me down memory lane over many cups of coffee, thank you for giving me another special memory. To my aunts and best friends, Paola and Franca, my gratitude for collecting family recipes.

Anna Garris began as my assistant and has become a dear friend. She sacrificed many hours for the sake of a deadline, even on Christmas Eve. Her dedication and organization skills came to my rescue on several occasions. Janet Fillmore, my editor at *The Plain Dealer*, spent many early mornings before going to work, proofreading and editing my recipes. Her confidence in this cookbook was contagious. Melissa DelGrosso and Kay Clark helped jump-start this entire project and assisted me in the creation of this cookbook's proposal.

Before a recipe can be included in any cookbook it must be tested and retested for perfection. Brenda Kelly is the ultimate sous chef. Through this testing, she has grown a true Italian heart and confesses a love for pasta and balsamic vinegar like no other. To my students and staff at the LPSC and their families, who also assisted in testing and tasting my recipes, a big *grazie*. Every Italian in Cleveland should befriend someone like Ray Gallucci. His assistance in getting the freshest Italian products was invaluable.

A special acknowledgment to my agent and friend, Jane Dystel, who believed in this project when it was still just an idea. Her encouragement and enthusiasm helped me along the way. No one has more patience than my editor, Melissa Jacobs. She believed so much in this cookbook that she bet her honeymoon on it. Evidence of her hard work can be seen on every page.

Introduction

There is more to a people than what is recorded in history books. Every day a person lives contains within it an epic of a journey complete with daily struggles and triumphs. At the end of that journey is a celebration, an evening meal. Each night's dinner is unique because it is a harmony of each family member's day, much as a recipe contains separate ingredients. These events are brought together to create that evening's feast. I grew up on those nightly creations. My cookbook is a celebration of those daily journeys.

I had the good fortune to be raised by two generations of Italian chefs. My mother had me shortly before opening her pasticceria/bar. With little time to raise a child and keep up with a blossoming career, my mother invoked the aid of her mother. I spent half my childhood in the professional kitchen of my mother, and the other half in the small traditional kitchen of my grandmother. I was raised in the best of both worlds.

I have distinctly different memories of each kitchen and of the dishes that evolved. My mother's kitchen was very bright, with stainless steel reflecting the white lights and white flour that seemed to dust the room. The dishes were equally bright and alive. There was a quiet perfection in everything my mother created.

My grandmother's kitchen had a softer lighting. Usually the only light in the kitchen came from beams of sunlight streaming through the sheer curtains framing the balcony window. The drying herbs hanging from the ceiling cast shadow islands in the sea of sunlight. Her dishes were equally warmer and softer.

The recipes I have gathered for *Bologna Mia: Memories from the Kitchen of Italy* evoke a memory as vivid for me as those kitchens of my childhood. Just as you might recall a memory from your childhood when you smell your mother's famous chocolate chip cookies baking in the oven, so each of these recipes comes with a story. This cookbook is a natural walk down memory lane for me. My Italian dishes come from the heart. My stories are true. On top of that, I had the good fortune to be born in the city of Bologna, known as the "Kitchen of Italy." The dishes I was raised on are considered by all Italians to be among the finest in Italy. It is these reputable recipes I offer.

This book brings the flavors of my city to you. I have had the fortune to travel all over the world, yet when I stand in the Piazza Maggiore in the heart of the city, I feel at peace, safe, and at home. But I am not alone in this feeling simply because Bologna is my home. Throughout Italy the Bolognese are called *simpatico*, meaning good-natured. Bolognese are known to be very hospitable, generous, and go out of their way to make visitors feel like family. It is this feeling of *family* I hope this cookbook shares with you.

The Bolognese also have a knack for taking simple ingredients and combining them to create uniquely flavorful dishes. They prefer simple recipes with fewer ingredients. However, the ingredients included in the recipes must be seasonably the best. This is evidenced in the amount of time the Bolognese spend at the market choosing only the ripest, freshest, and most flavorful items. This bright balance of flavor creates a tantalizing array of recipes.

Bologna is just starting to be recognized in the United States as a city of culinary importance. The trend is already starting in tours of Italy that now include a stop in Bologna, usually for lunch. Bologna's restaurants are alive with the energy of the city. The walls bounce with snippets of conversation and laughter. The service is impeccable because "good food should be enjoyed." The owner is always willing to share with you his latest find at the market. The *Sfogline*, or pasta ladies, are frequently the entertainment with their pasta tables placed in the window. This city celebrates the creation of a dish as much as the consumption. I want to share my pride in my city's heritage and growing reputation with you.

I recently lost both my grandmothers. This book is a tribute to them and the warm memories they gave me. It was a pleasure to recall the wonderful memories I have of the time I spent with them and share those stories with my family, some for the first time. It's funny how one story can open a floodgate of memories stored and almost forgotten. This cookbook has allowed me to capture those family traditions for the generations of my family to come. And like most family memories, the stories transcend bloodlines and can be embraced by others. I hope this cookbook creates for you the passion my family felt—and still feels—for food.

That passion has followed me into my professional life. As a chef and cooking teacher, I try to bring my enthusiasm for preparing simple yet flavorful dishes to my students. Having had the experience of being a culinary teacher for twenty years, I have had the opportunity to teach professional-level students as well as those who are just beginning the culinary arts. This experience has allowed me to write recipes that are quick, easy, and delicious. However, one does not need a culinary background to create these dishes. Most of the ingredients are easy to find and readily available in local markets.

This book is a unique project that took a lifetime to develop and one that can enrich any kitchen. I hope my recipes and memories can help you create some special dishes and remembrances of your own.

Chapter One

La Cucina della Città

Pomodori al Forno (*Oven-Roasted Stuffed Tomatoes*) Antipasto di Verdure (*Cold Vegetable Salad*) Frittelle di Baccalà (*Salt Cod Fritters*) Garganelli al Ragù Bianco (*Pasta with White Meat Sauce*)	**The Markets and the People of Bologna**
Pane Casareccio (*Hard Bread from Bologna*) Streghe (*Witches*) Grissini (*Breadsticks*) Ciambella Glassata (*Sweet Brioche Bread*) Crescente (*Bolognese Focaccia*)	**The Bread Shops of Bologna**
Gelato (*Italian Ice Cream*)	**Gelato**
Gnocchi di Patate (*Potato Dumplings*) Salsa alla Gorgonzola (*Cheese Sauce*) Filetto al Tartufo (*Beef Tenderloin with Truffle Sauce*) Cotolette alla Bolognese (*Veal Cutlets with Prosciutto and Cheese*)	**Restaurants of Bologna**

The Markets and the People of Bologna

Bologna is a small modern city with a rich culture, architectural treasures, and an impressive history. As an Etruscan stronghold with fertile farmland and hard-working people, the town was known as Felsina. It became a Roman city, Bononia, as a good omen to be expressed through the name "Bonus" in B.C. 189, second only in power to Rome. In 1530, Emperor Charles V was crowned in the church of San Petronio in Bologna. Bologna has always been a strong economic center for Italy. Located in the green valley of the Po River, the region is called "the bread basket" since most of the food grown in Italy comes from Emilia-Romagna. Bologna enjoys a perfect location that has inspired dreamers and lovers for thousands of years. Bologna is surrounded by the Apennine Mountains, near the Adriatic Sea and its beaches. The city's redbrick buildings, and the slender, tall silhouettes of Due Torri, the twin towers, bleed with color and light at sunset, and the city's thirty-five kilometers of porticos sparkle with life throughout the day.

A largely unknown destination to tourists traveling through Italy, nevertheless the city of Bologna has made significant contributions to the world: the oldest university in Europe, started nine hundred years ago; the famous Bolognese artist Ludovico Carracci; poets like Giosue Carducci; the father of modern medicine Marcello Malpighi; and Guglielmo Marconi, inventor of the radio; and, of course Bolognese cuisine. Bologna La Dotta (the learned) and Bologna La Grassa (the fat) is how an old saying describes the city, which perhaps best characterizes the city's harmonious blend of learning and good food.

To understand Bologna is to know its people. Bologna's warm hospitality and good nature is evident all over the city.

The unhurried pace of life and the impressive gastronomic reputation have made the Bolognese people very jolly and well loved throughout Italy.

Bologna is known as the kitchen of Italy. It is a prosperous city with a deep culinary heritage. This is evident in the sophisticated sidewalk cafés, the inviting bakeries, the elegant restaurants, and the colorful open-air markets. The markets are a feast for all senses, noisy and loud, and always bursting with people. With two center markets, Mercato di Via Clavature that spreads over three streets and the Mercato delle Erbe with over a hundred stalls called *treccole*, Bologna is a shopping shopper's fantasy realized. Vendors sell their specialties all year long: from seasonal ingredients, all sorts of fruits, vegetables, meat, game, fresh fish from the nearby sea, breads, pastas, to anything else that is edible. The vendors at the market always engage in colorful conversation with their customers about life, philosophy, politics, the economy, and of course sports. No need to buy a newspaper or watch television in Bologna; just go to the market and you will a feel part of the city's life. Bolognese go to the market not just to shop for their meal but to socialize, just as their forebears did during Roman times. Until the nineteenth century, the main square, Piazza Maggiore, was the main marketplace. Since the majority of the shoppers in those days could not read or write, they used ancient measures— "foot," "yard,": you can still see them etched in stone into the wall of city hall. Life in Bologna leaves behind the modern freneticism and chaos for espresso at dawn, and a steaming plate of tortellini at sunset with family and friends.

Pomodori al Forno

Oven-Roasted Stuffed Tomatoes

Serves 8

This recipe burst with tomato flavor! Roasting the tomatoes in the oven brings out their wonderful flavor. Use ripe seasonal tomatoes in summer or vine-ripe tomatoes in winter. At markets in Italy you can buy already roasted vegetables: onions, beets, potatoes, squash and pumpkin.

Steps and Procedures

1. Cut the tomatoes in half through the middle. With a spoon, scoop out the entire center including the seeds and put the pulp in a fine strainer. Press the pulp through with the back of a spoon. Reserve the tomato liquid mixture.

2. Sprinkle the tomato halves with ½ salt and 1 tablespoon olive oil, and set aside.

3. Line a 9-by-11-inch stainless-steel baking sheet with parchment paper. Preheat the oven to 350°F. In a small bowl mix, together the garlic, bread crumbs, ½ teaspoon salt and pepper, 2 tablespoons of the oil, parsley, cheese, the reserved tomato liquid and juice. Mix well and stuff the tomatoes with bread stuffing.

4. Place stuffed tomatoes on the prepared baking sheet. Drizzle with ½ tablespoon of the olive oil and bake at 350°F. for 35 to 40 minutes. Shake the pan every 15 minutes to prevent burning.

5. Drizzle with ½ teaspoon of oil before serving.

8 vine-ripe tomatoes
1 teaspoon sea salt
4 tablespoons extra-virgin olive oil
4 cloves garlic, peeled and coarsely chopped
1 cup fresh bread crumbs
Half teaspoon freshly ground black pepper
2 tablespoons fresh chopped Italian parsley
½ cup grated Parmigiano Reggiano cheese
¼ cup tomato juice

Antipasto di Verdure

Cold Vegetable Salad

Serves 6

1 firm fennel bulb
¼ cup fresh lemon
  juice
1 teaspoon Dijon
  mustard
1 teaspoon sea salt
½ teaspoon freshly
  grated black
  pepper
1 teaspoon chopped
  fresh Italian
  parsley
½ cup extra-virgin
  olive oil
2 stalks celery,
  trimmed
2 carrots, peeled
1 red pepper, cored
  and seeded
½ cup Parmigiano
  Reggiano, cut into
  slivers with a
  vegetable peeler

Shopping at the open-air markets in Bologna is a wonderful experience. Merchants become artists as they stack their fruits and vegetables up high in a multitude of colors, making them so inviting to buy. Late in the fall, finocchio, or fennel, an anise-flavored vegetable, is available. Buy a whole bulb, white in color and firm to the touch. Trim and wash it thoroughly, cut it up into quarters, and place it in cold water for an hour. This salad is also made with thin slices of white truffle. White truffles are found in the hills that surround Bologna and are located with the help of dogs or trained pigs. Vendors do not want to reveal their secret truffle location, so they set off in the middle of the night to gather their treasures. From the middle of September on, the markets in Bologna sell the fresh white truffles.

Steps and Procedures

1. Wash fennel, trim, and cut into quarters. Place in a bowl of cold water and set aside.
2. Whisk together lemon juice and mustard; add salt, pepper, and parsley.
3. Slowly whisk in olive oil to create an emulsion. Taste dressing and adjust seasoning.
4. Slice fennel, celery, carrots, and pepper very thin. Place in a large bowl, toss with dressing, and let the mixture marinate in the refrigerator for at least 30 minutes.
5. Transfer salad to a platter and sprinkle cheese on the top. Serve immediately.

Frittelle di Baccalà

Salt Cod Fritters

Serves 8

This dish is a must for Italian Christmas Eve celebrations. The whole meal is based on fish, and freshness is the number one requirement when buying seafood. In Bologna, they say if it doesn't move it is old. At the fish market there, you can see the fish moving in plastic tubs full of water. Make sure you buy fish without a fishy smell, with clear eyes, bright colors, firm flesh, fresh blood, and blood-red gills. Even if buying a fillet, be sure that it has a bright, vivid color. These little fritters are great as an appetizer. You can also substitute a variety of seafood (salmon, shrimp, tuna) for the salt cod, depending on what is fresh and available.

Steps and Procedures

1. Prepare cod by rinsing it well under cold running water. Transfer cod to the food processor and process to create a smooth mixture. Add the garlic, parsley, capers, and red pepper. Add the vinegar and process to incorporate, then add the eggs and bread crumbs.
2. Form and sauté 1 fritter to taste and season with salt and pepper to taste. Transfer mixture to a bowl, cover, and refrigerate for 20 minutes.
3. Heat oil in a large 12-inch frying pan. Add the cod mixture by the spoonful. Do not overcrowd.
4. Brown fritters on both sides, then drain on paper towels. Continue until all the mixture is used, taking care that the oil doesn't burn. Serve fritters with fresh tomato sauce (page 39).

2 pounds dried salt cod, already soaked in 8 cups whole milk for 3 days in the refrigerator

2 cloves garlic, peeled and minced

2 tablespoons fresh chopped Italian parsley

1 teaspoon capers

⅛ teaspoon crushed red pepper flakes

¼ cup white wine vinegar

2 large eggs

½ teaspoon freshly ground white pepper

Salt (optional)

1 cup canola or vegetable oil

2 cups of fresh bread crumbs

Garganelli al Ragù Bianco
Pasta with White Meat Sauce

Serves 8

White Meat Sauce

*1 carrot, peeled and
finely chopped*

*1 stalk celery, finely
chopped*

*1 small yellow onion,
peeled and finely
chopped*

*2 tablespoons extra-
virgin olive oil*

*1 pound lean ground
pork*

*¼ pound prosciutto,
finely chopped*

½ cup dry white wine

½ cup chicken stock

*1 tablespoon tomato
paste*

*1 cup heavy whipping
cream*

1 teaspoon sea salt

*¼ teaspoon freshly
ground white
pepper*

*Bologna's most famous delicatessen is Salsamenteria Tamburini,
which provides a true array of Bolognese specialties. Entering the store
is a celebration for all senses—prosciutto, mortadella, cotechino, and
salami are hanging from the ceiling and all manner of cheeses and balsamic vinegars are displayed. Glass showcases are brimming with
homemade pastas, hot and cold entrees, salads, and cooked vegetables.
In the back of the store, there is an open-fire rotisserie roasting chicken,
rabbits, and a variety of birds. I remember going there with my mother
as a child, and I couldn't wait to get home to open all the little packages.
My favorite was* squacquerone, *a soft creamy cheese that we always
spread over* crescentine, *a delicious fried dough. One of Tamburini's
talented cooks shared many recipes with me and it was difficult to pick
a favorite. I will admit, however, that the garganelli recipe is great. Garganelli are shaped like penne pasta, marked by using a special comb or
a wooden stick.*

Steps and Procedures

1. To make the sauce, in a 6 quart stockpot, cook the carrot,
   celery, and onion in olive oil until the onion is transparent.
   Add the pork and prosciutto and cook until brown. Add
   the wine and stock and cook until the wine evaporates.
   Add the tomato paste and cream to the mixture. Season
   with salt and pepper. Simmer for 45 minutes, stirring once
   in a while to prevent the sauce from sticking.
2. To make the dough, place the flour on a wooden board and
   form into a mound. Make a deep well in the center and
   break the eggs into it. Add the wine and salt. Use a fork to
   break up the eggs and mix the contents of the well.

3. Slowly add flour, beginning at top of the well so the walls collapse and blend into the mixture. When flour is almost totally absorbed, begin kneading, pressing with the palms of your hands. Knead the dough for about 20 minutes, until it is smooth and elastic. (If dough is dry, add a few drops of water. If sticky, add a sprinkle of flour.)

4. Gather the dough into a ball, place in a mixing bowl, and cover with plastic wrap. Let rest for 30 minutes. (To test for readiness, punch the dough with your index finger. If it springs back, it's done.)

5. Break the dough into lemon-size pieces and the feed pieces into pasta machine. Cut the dough into 2 inch squares and shape with the help of the comb for garganelli or wrap around a round stick to seal. Spread the garganelli out to dry on a parchment-lined cookie sheet.

6. Bring an 8 quart pot of water to boil. Add salt, asparagus tips, then pasta, and boil for 5 minutes. Drain and toss pasta with the white sauce.

7. Sprinkle garganelli with cheese and serve.

Pasta Dough

2 cups all-purpose
  flour
2 large eggs
¼ cup dry white wine
½ teaspoon sea salt
Salt
1 cup fresh asparagus
  tips
¼ cup grated
  Parmigiano
  Reggiano

The Bread Shops of Bologna

All cities in Italy have bread shops, but the Bolognese bread shops are unique. They not only sell breads but also a variety of homemade pastas, cookies, cakes, and even pizza. The glass windows display a variety of sugar confections, while the candies and the chocolates are always beautifully presented in tall glass vases with shining tops. Bolognese people are very fussy about their bread. There are more than one hundred and fifty different shapes of their *casareccio* (homemade) bread. It is denser and more flavorful than regular bread because of the higher flour content. Made with milk or an oil base, it requires a little muscle to knead it or a good electric machine. My favorite shop was the Simili bread shop. I would park my Motorino motorbike and my friends and I would each buy a piece of crescente, grissini, or pizza plus the daily bread for my family.

The daughters of the owner of the Simili bread shop, Margherita and Valeria run one of Bologna's finest cooking schools. They teach the art of bread making and Italian cooking to people from all over the world, and every year I bring groups of my students to them. We have so much fun cooking in their large kitchen. The Simili sisters are twins but they do not look at all alike. One is tall and the other is short, but they can anticipate each other's needs without words. A dynamic duo, they race around the large school kitchen as if on roller skates, calling their student's "darlings" and demanding attention by tapping the table or patting the students hands and constantly encouraging their progress. They are warm, friendly and very knowledgeable and after just one class you become part of the family. Through the years I have learned from them so much about baking and cooking, but most of all I have learned to be proud of my Bolognese heritage and my family. Here are several recipes from the Simili sisters that I have modified to suit my taste—and, I hope, yours.

Bolognese people are very fussy about their bread.

Pane Casareccio

Hard Bread from Bologna

Makes 4

Every morning the daily routine starts with Italian housewives going to the market to buy the day's provisions for their families. Dressed in their Sunday best with string bags under their arms, they hurry from one store to another, stopping from time to time to greet a friend. My favorite task was to buy bread for my family right after school. The sweet aroma of baking bread would fill the tiny shop always crowded with noisy customers.

Steps and Procedures

1. Proof the yeast in the water with the malt for 5 minutes until bubbles form on the top in a large glass bowl. Stir in the flour, cover with plastic wrap, and let the starter rest for at least 12 hours, or overnight, in a warm spot free from drafts.
2. Add the yeast to the starter and mix. Place the flour in the food processor, add the oil, salt, and starter. With the machine running, add only enough of the warm water to make a ball.
3. Knead the dough for 5 minutes. Remove and place it in an oiled bowl. Cover with plastic wrap and a thick towel and place in a warm spot to double in bulk.
4. Punch dough down; cut it into 4 pieces and shape into round rolls. Using a rolling pin, roll each of the rolls of dough flat as you would for pizza dough.
5. Starting at the long end, tightly roll up dough and seal by pinching it. Place on a parchment paper–lined cookie sheet. Repeat 3 more times. Let the bread rise for 30 to 40 minutes in a warm spot.

Starter

1 teaspoon active dry yeast

1 cup warm water (95° to 110°F.)

1 teaspoon malt

1 cup high-gluten bread flour

Dough

1 teaspoon active dry yeast

2 cups unbleached all-purpose flour

2 tablespoons extra-virgin olive oil

2 teaspoons sea salt

½ cup warm water (95° to 110°F.)

1 egg yolk mixed with 1 tablespoon water to make a glaze

6. Preheat the oven to 425°F. Just before baking, cut the top with a razor and brush with the egg glaze. Bake for 15 minutes, then reduce the heat to 375°F. and bake for an additionally 30 minutes. Gently tap the bottom of the breads and if you hear an hollow sound remove the breads from the oven.

7. Cool breads on a wire rack, for 20 minutes before serving.

Streghe

Witches

Serves 12

Make plenty of "witches" because there are never enough of them to go around. These treats were originally made by the bakers to test their oven in the morning to see if the oven was hot enough to bake bread. Usually the baker would be the only one to enjoy the witches, but since they became so popular, now they are made all day long so everyone can enjoy them.

2 teaspoon active dry yeast
1½ cups warm water (95° to 110°F.)
1 teaspoon granulated sugar
4½ cups unbleached all-purpose flour
¼ cup vegetable shortening
2 teaspoons sea salt plus extra for seasoning witches
Vegetable oil

Steps and Procedures

1. Proof the yeast in warm water, add the sugar, and stir until bubbles form. Place the flour, salt, and shortening in the food processor, and with the machine running add the proofed yeast.

2. Work the dough for 5 minutes. Add more warm water or flour as needed. Remove the dough from the machine. Knead by hand for 5 minutes; it should feel smooth and elastic. Place the dough in a greased bowl, cover with plastic wrap, and then let it rest for about 45 to 50 minutes in a warm spot.

3. Preheat the oven to 400°F. Brush a baking sheet with vegetable oil.

4. Take a little piece of dough about the size of an egg, and, without kneading, flatten it until very thin with a hand-crank pasta machine set to the last setting. Put it on the oiled sheet, stretch it a little with your hands, brush it with oil mixed with salt, then cut into a diamond shape. Continue the process until all the dough is used.

5. Bake immediately in the preheated oven for 8 to 10 minutes, or until lightly golden brown.

Grissini
Breadsticks
Makes 24

2 teaspoons active dry
  yeast
1 teaspoon granulated
  sugar
1 cup warm water
  (95° to 110°F.)
6 tablespoons extra-
  virgin olive oil
2½ cups high-gluten
  bread flour
2 teaspoons sea salt

Making breadsticks is so easy and so much fun. Prepare the bread dough and then shape it into long, thin ropes. Brush them with oil and bake until golden brown. My daughters and I love making them in a variety of flavor and shapes.

Steps and Procedures
1. In a bowl, dissolve the yeast and the sugar in the water. Proof until bubbles form.
2. Stir in 2 tablespoons of the olive oil; add the flour and 1 teaspoon of the salt. Add more flour or water as needed.
3. Place the dough on the table; flour surface and knead well for a few minutes. Place the dough in an oiled bowl covered with plastic wrap and let it rise in a warm spot until it is doubled in bulk (at least 1 hour).
4. Punch the dough down. Roll out the dough into a 14-by-4-inch rectangle. Press the dough down with the palm of your hands. Brush with olive oil, sprinkle with salt, cover. Let the dough rest for 1 hour.
5. Preheat the oven to 400°F.
6. From the short side of the rectangle cut the dough into strips about the size of one fat finger. Place on a parchment-lined baking sheet, stretching the dough slightly and pressing the ends onto the sheet pan so they will stick.
7. Bake in the preheated oven for 20 minutes, or until golden brown.

Ciambella Glassata

Sweet Brioche Bread

Serves 12

Brioche is the famous rich yeast dough with a tender crust achieved by working a maximum amount of butter and eggs into the dough. It can be formed into classic shapes like this one for ciambella glassata, also known as polacca or angelica. Fermentation for this rich dough is slower than with leaner yeast dough. All ingredients except the butter should be at room temperature before making the dough. In her bakery my mother made them as individual rolls and filled some with pastry cream. These were my husband's favorite, and you know what they say about the way to a man's heart—these definitely helped. He used to come to the pasticceria early in the morning so he could get them right out of the oven.

Steps and Procedures

1. Boil the milk first to kill the enzymes and then cool to 95° to 110°F.
2. Preheat the oven to 400°F. Proof the yeast in warm milk with 1 teaspoon sugar until bubles form. Place the flour and salt into the food processor. Add the lemon zest, vanilla, and eggs.
3. With the machine running, add the proofed yeast. Work the dough for 10 minutes, adding more warm milk or flour as needed. Cut the butter into small pieces and beat just until the dough is smooth and the butter is incorporated.
4. Remove and place the dough in a buttered bowl. Cover with plastic wrap and a towel. Place bowl in a warm spot to doubled in bulk about 1 hour.
5. Punch the dough down and allow to rise again for another hour, or until doubled in bulk.

Dough

2 teaspoons active dry yeast

1 cup warm milk (95° to 110°F.)

1 teaspoon granulated sugar

4 cups unbleached all-purpose flour

1 teaspoon sea salt

1 teaspoon lemon zest

1 teaspoon vanilla sugar or vanilla extract

3 large eggs

8 tablespoons unsalted butter, softened

See page 16 for Filling Ingredients

Filling

8 tablespoon butter, melted

½ cup granulated sugar

1 cup golden raisins soaked in ¼ cup rum

¼ cup toasted sliced almonds

1 teaspoon lemon zest

Egg glaze prepared with 1 egg yolk mixed with 1 tablespoon water

8 tablespoons confectioners' sugar plus 1 teaspoon lemon juice, mixed well together, to make a glaze

6. Place the dough on the work surface and roll it out into a 9-by-15-inch rectangle.

7. Brush the dough with melted butter and spread with raisins, almonds, lemon zest, and sugar.

8. Fold the dough in half. Cut the dough into 3 equal pieces. Roll each piece into a long rope.

9. Braid the dough. Place the braid on a parchment-lined cookie sheet and shape it into a wreath. Pinch the ends together to maintain the shape of the braid.

10. Brush the braid with melted butter set in a warm place until doubled in bulk.

11. Bake for 15 minutes in the preheated 400°F. oven. Lower the heat to 350°F. and bake for another 30 minutes, to ensure that the ciambella is golden brown yet hollow in the middle. To test for doneness, turn the ciambella upside down and gently tap it—you will hear a hollow sound.

12. Remove the ciambella from the oven. Cool for 1 hour, brush with the prepared glaze, and allow to dry before serving.

Crescente

Bolognese Focaccia

(Makes 1 Crescente)

La Crescente Bolognese is made in sheet pans and comes plain or in a variety of flavors: fresh herb, prosciutto, pancetta, ciccioli, and cheese. It is eaten all through the day, for breakfast or a snack or even as bread. We make it at my school every day, using the food processor. Every student always asks for the recipe.

1 cup warm water (95° to 110°F.)

2 teaspoons active dry yeast

1 teaspoon granulated sugar

2½ cups high-gluten bread flour

2 teaspoons sea salt

¼ cup extra-virgin olive oil plus extra oil to brush jelly-roll pan and top of dough

1 teaspoon fresh chopped rosemary

¼ cup prosciutto, finely minced

Steps and Procedures

1. Place the warm water in the food processor, stir in the yeast and sugar and cover. Let it proof for 10 minutes in a warm spot.
2. Add 1 cup of the flour, 1 teaspoon of the salt and the olive oil to the food processor. Pulse 4 or 5 pulses times.
3. Add the remaining flour, rosemary, and prosciutto. Work the dough in the processor until smooth and elastic. (Add more flour or water as needed).
4. Let dough rise until doubled bulk in the sealed food processor bowl. Punch the dough down and roll it out into a 10-by-14-inch rectangle. Oil a jelly-roll pan and add the prepared dough.
5. With a fork, make markings, and with the fat part of your finger, press down on the dough to make dimples. Allow the dough to rise again. Preheat the oven to 400°F.
6. Brush with oil and the remaining salt. Bake for 20 minutes until light golden in color.
7. Let it cool on a wire rack and cut it into 2-by-2 pieces.
8. Serve warm!

Gelato

*T*he sight of a scrumptious cone of ice cream can make us all turn into children. When we walk in front of an ice-cream parlor, we can't resist stopping in for a taste. Our hearts start to beat faster, our minds fill with happy memories, our eyes feast on the many colors of the delicious flavors and our taste buds can't wait for that first cool bite. Personally, I've always had a passion for eating ice cream, and remember it as a delicious and refreshing part of many hot summer days. I can remember with a touch of nostalgia the many Sunday afternoons as a child in Italy when we would go to the center of town and join the many people leisurely strolling and stopping at the many kiosks or at the fancy parlors where we would sit under the big umbrellas, eating ice cream and watching the people pass by.

My family's favorite parlor was Gelateria Da Pino, famous all over as the best gelato maker in Bologna. In Italy, ice cream making is still considered an art, passed down from generation to generation. Using only the freshest ingredients — eggs, cream, sugar, flavoring, and fruit — the Italians create a luscious product that has won the praise of aficionados around the world. Gelato, as ice cream is called in Italy, is different from its American counterpart in that it has less air, a custard base, and a higher butterfat content, making it creamier and smoother.

Where did gelato come from, you may ask. It does come from Italy, but its history will surprise you. Gelato had a very humble beginning. During the Roman invasions, soldiers in between battles used to refresh themselves with snow flavored with fruit juices or honey. History books tell us that during the Nero Empire, even the athletes enjoyed this cool refreshment. Though nothing like ice cream, it was very similar to what we know today as snow cones.

An architect, Bernardo Buontalenti, introduced the first real ice cream to the Medici court in Florence. He didn't leave many famous buildings, but he did leave something much better. He discovered that by immersing custard in ice and salt and stirring it for a while, the liquid turned solid. Though his invention of ice cream certainly brought wealth and fame in his lifetime, I can't help but wonder if he had any idea how big his little creation would become.

Contrary to popular belief, it wasn't Caterina de' Medici who introduced this treat to France when she married King Henry II, but instead it was a poor Sicilian immigrant named Francesco Procopio who did so in 1660. In the United States, a Genoese immigrant first introduced ice cream in 1770, when he opened the first ice cream parlor. Fame and fortune followed ice cream everywhere it went.

In Italy, even today ice cream is considered a summer enjoyment, while here in the United States we eat ice cream every hour of the day in every season, hot or cold. Nothing stops us from enjoying it. This is probably why we hold the record for eating the most ice cream in the world, over sixty pounds per person per year; that translates into one scoop per day per person and makes us the world's largest manufacturer of ice cream.

Given Americans great love for ice cream, it is only natural that we would invent the ice cream cone. During the World's Fair in St. Louis, vendors noticed that people dipped their waffles into their ice cream. They soon discovered that by rolling the waffles into a conelike shape, they could place the ice cream right inside.

There are three categories of cream, each made from a different bases. First is the custard base used for making gelato, the second is the milk base used for making most ice cream in United States, and the third is a sugar syrup used for making sorbet. It really doesn't matter what ingredients you use when you make your ice cream, just make sure to use the freshest ones and the final product will be absolutely delicious.

In Italy, ice cream making is still considered an art, passed down from generation to generation.

Ice cream making has become very simple today. Long gone is the old-fashioned method of hand stirring. Electric machines with a cooling motor built right in have made ice cream making a breeze. There's nothing more rewarding than making ice cream at home. I know my daughters don't agree with me on this point because they feel the best part is eating the ice cream.

Gelato
Italian Ice Cream
Serves 6

This is a great gelato recipe, so easy to make and so delicious because of the wonderful vanilla flavor. This is my family's favorite ice cream recipe. Use it as a base for your own favorite gelato, and then add cocoa, fresh fruit, nuts, or chocolate. Use an electric ice cream maker with a built-in cooling unit, even an old-fashioned one. The whole family will enjoy this delicious treat.

2 cups whole milk or half-and-half
1 vanilla bean, crushed
1 teaspoon vanilla extract
1 piece lemon peel
6 large egg yolks
1 cup granulated sugar

Steps and Procedures

1. Heat the milk in a 2-quart saucepan with the vanilla bean and extract and the lemon peel until it reaches below the boiling point. In a mixing bowl, beat the yolks until pale yellow and smooth, add the sugar, and whisk until thoroughly combined.

2. Temper the mixture by whisking ½ cup of the hot milk into the egg mixture. Place the custard back on the stove and cook over medium heat, whisking for 10 minutes. Remove the custard from the stove and place in a small bowl. Cover with plastic wrap. Refrigerate to chill for at least 2 hours.

3. Pour the mixture through a strainer into ice-cream maker and chill according to the manufacturer's directions.

4. Serve gelato with fresh berries or fruit. In Bologna they serve gelato with amarene Fabbri—wild cherries in a delicious sauce.

The Restaurants of Bologna

What do you think the restaurants of a culinary city like Bologna are like? From elegant and sophisticated restaurants to plain and simple trattorias, they are wonderful of course. Most of the restaurants look charming as they spill out under the city's porticos, with tables and chairs nestled in little makeshift gardens, or taking over narrow side streets with large umbrellas covering the tables. Menus vary from traditional Bolognese cuisine to modern cuisine with an international twist. The restaurants always seem to be crowded and noisy and have with a partylike atmosphere. Most of them, however, have an exceptional waitstaff ready to accommodate every demand. A large number of the eateries are family-run and have been around so long that they have become part of the city's folklore. Restaurants like Pappagallo, Da Rodrigo, Buca di S. Petronio, Diana, Da Gianni, Cesarina, and Cesoia are just a few of the many wonderful Bolognese institutions that have helped continue the tradition of Bolognese cooking at its best.

Going out for dinner was always very special, because our family would usually have a *tavolata*, a long narrow table where family members would usually meet. Having a large family meant that when we got together we would take over the restaurant. My mother would always bring the dessert, and it would always be placed on a dessert cart and wheeled out at the end of the dinner, in the midst of accolades from all the guests. How proud I was of my mamma. This was the time to visit with family and friends and share a good meal and catch up on the details of everyone's life. It was such fun to be served family-style and watch dishes of all sorts be placed before you. This is what I miss the most when I think of Italy—my family and friends, the big tavolata, and the great meals that we shared.

Gnocchi di Patate

Potato Dumplings

Serves 8

My favorite little potato dumplings, gnocchi, are from a wonderful restaurant in Bologna called Da Rodrigo, a Bolognese institution where the food and the service are impeccable. Signor Giancarlo, the owner, is a true buongustaio *and oversees all the activity of the restaurant. I had the pleasure of working in his kitchen and here are the recipes that he shared. Gnocchi is the easiest homemade pasta of all. It can be lots of fun if done with a friend. Make it fresh on the day that you plan to serve it since gnocchi do not freeze well. I add a little baking powder to the dough to make the dumplings lighter.*

2½ pounds Idaho potatoes
2 large eggs
1 teaspoon sea salt
Salsa alla Gorgonzola (recipe follows)
2 tablespoons grated Parmigiano Reggiano cheese
1 teaspoon baking powder
2½ cups all-purpose flour

Steps and Procedures

1. Scrub the potatoes. Place them with their jackets on in a 6-quart pot of water and boil until fork-tender, about 30 minutes.
2. Drain the water from the potatoes, then cool in pot. Peel and rice potatoes (use a ricer, not a food processor). Cool for at least 30 minutes.
3. Make a well with the riced potatoes. Add the eggs, salt, baking powder, and three-quarters of the flour to the middle of the well. Slowly combine the mixture with the potatoes to make a dough. Do not overwork the dough or it will become heavy. Add the remaining flour, only if needed. The dough should be smooth but not sticky.
4. Cut the dough into 5 equal pieces. On a floured surface, use your palms to roll each piece into a long tube. Use a dough cutter to cut each tube into one-inch-long pieces. Dust gnocchi with flour and place on a gnocchi maker or the back of a fork or a grater. Roll each piece, pressing

with your thumb in the center of each to give it the classic dimple in the center.

5. Bring an 8-quart pot of water to a boil. Cook the gnocchi for 3 minutes. (Once the gnocchi come to the surface of the water, let them cook for 2 more minutes and then remove them with a slotted spoon to a platter.) Toss the gnocchi with Salsa alla Gorgonzola, sprinkle with grated cheese and serve.

Salsa alla Gorgonzola
Cheese Sauce

Makes 2 cups

½ pint (1 cup) heavy cream
2 tablespoons unsalted butter
¼ pound freshly grated sweet Gorgonzola cheese
2 tablespoons freshly grated Parmigiano Reggiano cheese
⅛ teaspoon freshly grated ground nutmeg
1 teaspoon sea salt
½ teaspoon freshly ground white pepper
¼ cup chopped toasted walnuts

Steps and Procedures

1. In a 12-inch saucepan, bring cream and butter to a boil. Reduce at high heat until the mixture thickens, about 10 minutes.
2. Stir in the cheeses and cook until well melted. Season with nutmeg, salt, and pepper.
3. Pour over the gnocchi di patate, sprinkle with walnuts, and serve.

Filetto al Tartufo

Beef Tenderloin with Truffle Sauce

Serves 8

Buy a whole vacuum-packed tenderloin. Remove all the outside fat by hand. Using a sharp boning knife, completely clean the filet of remaining fat and trim away any sinew. Remove the chain muscle (the long piece of meat alongside the filet) and reserve it. Insert the knife under the silver-skin, the white connective tissue that covers the muscle; pull one end of the silver-skin and scrape it away from the meat.

1 whole beef tenderloin

1 tablespoon white truffle oil

1 teaspoon freshly ground black pepper

See page 26 for Truffle Sauce Ingredients

Steps and Procedures

1. In a small 3-quart saucepan, melt the butter and gently cook the chain meat, celery, onion, and carrot until the onion starts to caramelize. Add the tomatoes, bay leaf, stock, and port wine. Raise the heat to high and allow the liquid to reduce by half. Taste for seasoning. Reduce the heat to low and gently simmer the sauce for 30 minutes.

2. To cook the tenderloin, fold the tail of the filet under and tie with butcher string to help make the filet cook evenly. Preheat oven to 500°F. Rub the tenderloin all over with truffle oil, season with pepper, and roast for 20 minutes. Season with salt and pepper and reduce the heat to 350°F. and let the tenderloin cook for an additional 15 more minutes. The temperature must reach 120° to 130°F. for rare on a meat thermometer.

3. Strain the sauce in the saucepan directly into a sauté pan to deglaze. Press down hard on the solids to extract as much flavor as possible. Set the sauté pan over high heat and scrape up any bits of flavor clinging to the bottom of

Truffle Sauce

2 tablespoons
    unsalted butter
1 small onion, peeled
    and minced
1 small carrot, peeled
    and minced
1 stalk celery, finely
    minced
1 cup seeded and
    chopped ripe Roma
    tomatoes
1 bay leaf
1 cup reduced beef
    stock
1 cup port wine
1 teaspoon sea salt
$\frac{1}{2}$ teaspoon freshly
    ground black
    pepper
2 tablespoons softened
    unsalted butter for
    mounting the sauce
Truffle shavings
    (optional)

the pan. Bring the sauce to a boil and reduce slightly to concentrate the flavors. Taste and adjust the seasoning.

4. Place the tenderloin on a serving platter. While the sauce is boiling, whisk in the softened butter bit by bit. Ladle the sauce over the tenderloin and sprinkle with truffle shavings. Serve immediately.

Cotolette alla Bolognese

Veal Cutlets with Prosciutto and Cheese

Serves 8

This recipe is a classic of the Bolognese cuisine. In Bologna the best veal cutlets, along with many other super recipes, are served at a wonderful restaurant called Buca S. Petronio. After 30 years in business, it has become a Bolognese institution. The head chef, Signora Clara, is an energetic lady who makes everything from scratch, taking advantage of the best seasonal ingredients, since the restaurant is next to the main open food market. I have enjoyed many great meals there under the porticos, and have had the pleasure to spend time in the kitchen with Signora Clara.

Steps and Procedures

1. In a small bowl, beat together the eggs, milk, nutmeg, and half the salt and pepper.

2. In another small bowl mix together the bread crumbs, cheese, and the remaining salt and pepper.

3. With a flat meat mallet, pound the veal between pieces of plastic wrap. Dip each cutlet first in the egg mixture, then dip in the bread crumb mixture. Make sure that the coating is secure by pressing down on the cutlet. Repeat this step until all the cutlets are done. Refrigerate until ready to cook. Preheat the oven at 350°F.

4. Heat the oil in a 12-inch frying pan, add a couple of cutlets at the time, and cook until golden brown on both sides. Drain on paper towels.

5. Place the cutlets on a sheet pan. Top each with a slice of prosciutto and one of cheese.

6. Bake in the oven for 10 to 15 minutes, or until the cheese is melted.

3 large eggs
½ cup whole milk
⅛ teaspoon freshly grated nutmeg
1 teaspoon sea salt
½ teaspoon freshly grated black pepper
3 cups fresh bread crumbs seasoned
½ cup freshly grated Parmigiano Reggiano cheese
8 thin slices veal scaloppini, best from the leg top round
2 tablespoons olive oil
8 thin slices prosciutto di Parma
8 thin slices fontina cheese

Chapter Two

La Cucina della Nonna Luisa

Tortellini in Brodo (*Tortellini in Broth*)
Al Brodo (*Broth*)
Tortelloni alla Gorgonzola (*Fat Cheese Tortelloni*)

Nonna Luisa's History of Tortellini

Lasagne Verdi alla Bolognese (*Lasagne Bolognese Style*)
Galantina alla Galantini (*Boneless Stuffed Capon*)
Zuppa Inglese (*English Trifle*)
Croccante (*Hazelnut Brittle*)

Christmas at Nonna Luisa's

Polenta ai Funghi (*Polenta with Mushroom Sauce*)
Osso Buco (*Braised Veal Shanks*)
Salsiccia e Fagioli (*Sausage and Beans*)
Pollo della Nonna (*Grandmother's Chicken*)
Peperonata (*Spicy Pepper Salad*)

"Smoked" Polenta

La Ieda (*Pasta with Walnut Sauce*)
Frittata di Erbette (*Herb Omelet*)
Arrosto di Maiale alle Albicocche
(*Apricot-Stuffed Roast Pork Loin*)
Pollo ai Funghi Porcini (*Chicken Breasts with
Porcini Mushroom Sauce*)
Zuccherini Montanari (*Wedding Cookies*)

Summer in the Country

Life, Love, and Family

Tagliatelle al Prosciutto (*Pasta with Prosciutto Sauce*)
Gramigna alla Salsiccia (*Pasta with Sausage*)
Carpaccio di Funghi (*Marinated Portobello Mushrooms*)
Faraona al Forno (*Oven-Roasted Guinea Hens*)
Spezzatino con Piselli e Patate
(*Veal Stew with Peas and Potatoes*)
Castagnaccio di Uvetta e Pinoli
(*Chestnut Flat Bread with Raisins and Pine Nuts*)

Nonna Luisa's History of Tortellini

Sunday mornings were always the busiest for my parents in the pasticceria; therefore I would spend my Sunday morning at my Nonna Luisa's house helping to prepare for the big family banquet that afternoon. Sundays were busy at Nonna Luisa's as well. My cousins and I, all of us girls, would gather around my grandmother's big wooden table to begin our weekly chore.

Nonna had risen hours earlier and created the dough and filling for that day's tortellini. She had already spread out the dough on the table, rolling it very thin. Then she had carefully placed a spoonful of the filling in the center of each square.

Our job was to take each little square and wrap it around our tiny fingers to create the tortellini. We would spend hours shaping tortellini, partly because they were so small it took quite a few to feed our large family, and partly because when Nonna wasn't looking we children would shove as many raw tortellini in our mouths as possible. In hindsight, she must have known our trick, as we would continue talking with squirrel cheeks full of dough.

We discussed everything that was important to us—toys, school, boys, and the beach. Nonna always listened to whatever tales we might share. When we tired of talking we would turn to Nonna, who always seemed to have a great new story of her past we had never heard. My favorite was one about Bologna's past. It was the story of the creation of tortellini. Verona might have Romeo and Juliet, but we Bolognese had tortellini! I can hear my grandmother's voice as I share this story with you.

Once upon a time in Bologna lived many wealthy families. These families were very jealous and constantly tried to top each other. When one family built a tower in town, all the others raced to build a taller tower. Many of those towers still stand in the center of town.

When one family had a great chef, the others searched for a

La Cucina della Nonna Luisa

31

better one. This is where our story begins. One such family hired a new chef. He was a young, handsome man with a great knack for pasta. At this time all the other families' chefs were busy creating new sauces. So this wealthy man, not to be out-done, called his chef to his great banquet hall.

"I demand a new sauce for my pasta," bellowed the wealthy man.

"I will try to create a new sauce," replied the chef humbly, "but there are so many new ones out there how will I know if I have created one not yet invented?"

"Good point," grumbled the wealthy man, "you must then create a new pasta."

The chef was stunned. A new pasta—was it possible? Right at that moment, the large doors at the end of the banquet hall squeaked open and in walked the most beautiful woman the chef had ever seen. She was so lovely that he fell in love with her instantly. He bowed to the wealthy man and then to the wealthy man's beautiful wife and hurried out of the hall to the kitchen.

The chef was in a great turmoil. He was too much in love to care about creating a new pasta for his master. He wanted only to worship the wife. He thought of declaring his love to her, but he did not know how. Months went by and the chef was still consumed by thought of his master's lady. He thought of paint-ing her portrait, but he was no Michelangelo. He thought of composing music about her, but he was no Paganini either. The only thing that he was good at was cooking, but how could he confess his love to this woman through food? He made the most incredible sauces, the most delicate desserts, but she never real-ized those masterpieces held such a special message.

Meanwhile, the wealthy man was getting impatient. Although he enjoyed the wonderful dishes his chef brought out nightly, he was anxious to serve new pasta. He called the chef back into the banquet hall the next day.

"I have invited all the wealthiest families of Bologna to my table this evening. I expect you to serve a new pasta or I will throw you out of my house!" The chef was ready to collapse. If he were thrown out of the house he would never get to see the

A new pasta —

was it possible?

beautiful wife again. With his head hung low, he started to return to his kitchen when he heard laughter coming from his lady's chamber. The chef tiptoed toward her door, opened it slightly, and peaked in.

The room was filled with bubbles. They floated around the chamber popping on various statues and furniture. He traced their origin to a large tub in the corner of the room by the fireplace. In the tub surrounded by bubbles sat the beautiful wife. She was so involved in her bath and the bubbles that she did not notice the chef watching her from the doorway. He watched her intently trying to remember every detail of her body fearing he might never see her after tonight's banquet.

Suddenly feeling a draft, the wife stood up from her bath and robed herself. The chef gasped at what he saw and ducked out of the room before she realized the draft came from the open doorway where he stood. As he raced down the hallway toward the kitchen, he marveled at what he had just seen. This woman had the most unique belly button he had ever seen. He wanted to immortalize it and in doing so declare his love for her.

He feverishly set to work. Banning everyone from the kitchen, he slaved over dough, twisting and turning it, trying to recapture that beautiful sight. It wasn't until the guests had already started to arrive for the banquet that he finally found the perfect technique.

The wealthy man tapped his fingers on the great table nervously. He had heard rumors that the chef had closed himself in the kitchen all day. He hoped that the chef had discovered some great new pasta that would make him the wealthiest, most respected man in all of Bologna. The table servants soon arrived carrying great silver trays with ornate covers. The wealthy man looked toward the doors, and standing just beyond them was the chef, nervously wringing his hands.

The wealthy man looked down at the tray before him and with a quick intake of breath lifted the cover to display his new pasta. His wife gasped in horror. The wealthy man, recognizing the form of his wife's belly button, shook with anger and motioned

Banning everyone from the kitchen, he slaved over dough, twisting and turning it, trying to recapture that beautiful sight.

for the chef to enter the room. As the chef approached, he kept his eyes on the wife, who looked at him in disbelief.

"Explain yourself!" said the master in a low voice checked filled with fury.

"I am in love with your wife," answered the chef. "I wanted to immortalize her. What better way than as a new pasta as you requested."

The guests whispered frantically about what this all meant. They stared down at their plates at the delicious-looking little pastas and then back at the scene before them.

"Guards!" screamed the wealthy man. He had the chef beheaded while standing there.

The wife began to sob, knowing the poor chef died only because he was in love with her. The wealthy man, already feeling betrayed by his chef, mistook her tears as those shed for a lost lover and ordered his wife beheaded as well.

The guests stared in disbelief at the two bodies on the floor. The wealthy man had tried to kill the love his chef felt by killing him and his own wife, but as the guests looked back at their still-warm plates they realized that the love the chef felt would stay alive as long as people still made his pasta. To this day when a couple eats tortellini together it is said they will be in love forever.

This chapter focuses on my father's mother's kitchen. She was the pasta expert in my family. Her dishes were always accompanied by great stories of her childhood and Bologna's past.

Tortellini in Brodo

Tortellini in Broth

Serves 8

Tortellini are the superstars of Bolognese pasta; every family has its own secret recipe. In Italy, tortellini are always meat-filled. Tortelloni are cheese-filled. Make sure that you place the tortellini on parchment paper or on a clean cotton cloth, refrigerate them until ready to cook, or freeze them well sealed. Cook tortellini in broth, not in water, or their flavor will be lost. Capon broth is the best. Traditionally tortellini are served in cream sauce "alla Panna" or in a tomato meat sauce, or in broth, the preferred Bolognese way.

Steps and Procedures

1. To make the dough, place the flour on a wooden board and form into a mound. Make a deep well in the center and break the eggs into it. Add the wine and salt. Use a fork to break up the eggs and mix the contents of the well.
2. Slowly add flour, beginning at the top of the well so that the walls collapse and blend into the mixture. When the flour is almost totally absorbed, begin kneading, pressing with the palms of your hands. Knead the dough for about 20 minutes, until it becomes smooth and elastic. (If the dough is dry, add a few drops of water. If it is sticky, add a sprinkle of flour.)
3. Gather the dough into a ball, place in a mixing bowl, cover with plastic wrap, and let rest at room temperature for 30 minutes. (To test for readiness, punch the dough with your index finger. If it springs back, it is done.)
4. To make the filling, sauté the chicken and the pork in oil in a 12-inch frying pan for 5 minutes on each side. Cool slightly. Place the meat in the food processor with the pro-

Pasta Dough

3 cups all-purpose flour, preferably unbleached
3 large eggs
¼ cup dry white wine
1 teaspoon sea salt
Water or extra flour, if needed

See page 36 for Filling Ingredients

Filling

1 whole boneless and skinless chicken breast
½ pound boneless pork loin
2 tablespoons extra-virgin olive oil
¼ pound prosciutto
¼ pound mortadella bologna
¼ cup grated Parmigiano Reggiano cheese
2 large eggs
½ teaspoon freshly ground nutmeg

½ teaspoon sea salt
½ teaspoon freshly ground black pepper
1 egg yolk plus 1 tablespoon water mixed together to make an egg wash
12 cups broth—Il Brodo (recipe on page 37)
Freshly grated Parmigiano Reggiano cheese for garnish

sciutto and mortadella and process until smooth. Add the cheese, eggs, nutmeg, salt and pepper and incorporate with the meat mixture. Place the filling in a small bowl, cover with plastic wrap, and refrigerate until ready to use.

5. Break the pasta dough into lemon-size pieces. Shape each piece into a long, thin sheet. Cut the sheet into small strips, 1 inch wide, then into little squares, about 1 inch square. Place ½ teaspoon of meat filling on each square and shape immediately into a triangle. Seal edges securely, using a little egg wash if necessary to make it stick. Hold the triangle in your right hand and fold it around your left index finger so that the two ends curl around and overlap each other. Repeat until all squares are done.

6. Spread the tortellini out to dry on a parchment-lined cookie sheet, making sure they do not touch. In a 6-quart pot boil the tortellini in the prepared broth for 5 to 7 minutes. Taste for seasoning. Serve with freshly grated cheese.

Il Brodo

All-Purpose Techniques for Stock Making

Makes 12 cups

Slow and long cooking and good, flavorful ingredients are the perfect combinations for a good-quality stock. Use cold water and no salt. Skim the foamy impurities from the surface. To prevent cloudiness, do not stir the stock. Stock may be reduced by half and frozen in ice cube trays, then bagged for quick sauce making or pan deglazing. Stock may be reduced further for an intense glace de viande *meat glaze. Meat bones for stock can be purchased over the counter in large supermarkets. Or call the meat department ahead and reserve them. Veal bones add body to the stock—don't omit them.*

Steps and Procedures

1. Place the veal and capon in a large 12-quart stockpot; cover with cold water and slowly bring liquid to a rapid boil. Skim the scum as it rises to the surface.

2. Lower the heat to a simmer, add the vegetables, parsley, and the bay leaf. Cook the stock very gently, skimming occasionally, for 3 hours. Extract the veal bones and remove the capon and reserve it for another use, store it in the refrigerator. Cool the stock for 30 minutes in a sink filled with ice water before straining.

3. Strain the stock through a fine strainer lined with cheesecloth. Refrigerate overnight for easy removal of fat from the surface. Transfer the defatted stock to a container and refrigerate for up to 1 week or freeze for up to 2 months.

*1 pound veal knuckle
and neck bones
1 capon (3–4
pounds), cleaned
4 quarts cold water, to
cover the
ingredients in the
stockpot by 1 inch
1 carrot, chopped
1 large onion, peeled
and chopped
2 celery ribs with
leaves chopped
8 parsley sprigs
1 bay leaf*

Tortelloni alla Gorgonzola

Fat Cheese Tortelloni

Serves 8

Pasta Dough

3 cups all-purpose flour, preferably unbleached
3 large eggs
¼ cup dry white wine
1 teaspoon sea salt
Water or extra flour, if needed

Filling

¼ cup grated Parmigiano Reggiano cheese
1 pound fresh whole milk ricotta cheese
¼ pound Gorgonzola cheese, crumbled
2 large eggs
½ teaspoon freshly ground nutmeg
1 teaspoon sea salt
½ teaspoon freshly ground black pepper

This is my grandmother's recipe. She made these for my husband all the time when we lived in Italy, because they are his favorite. Before I moved to the United States, she taught me the recipe so he could enjoy them here.

Steps and Procedures

1. To make the dough, place the flour on a wooden board and form into a mound. Make a deep well in the center and break the eggs into it. Add the wine and salt. Use a fork to break up the eggs and mix the contents of the well.
2. Slowly add flour, beginning at the top of the well so that the walls collapse and blend into the mixture. When the flour is almost totally absorbed, begin kneading, pressing with the palms of your hands. Knead the dough for about 20 minutes, until it becomes smooth and elastic. (If the dough is dry, add a few drops of water. If it is sticky, add a sprinkle of flour.)
3. Gather the dough into a ball, place it in a mixing bowl, cover with plastic wrap, and let rest at room temperature for 30 minutes. (To test for readiness, punch the dough with your index finger. If it springs back, it is done.)
4. To make the filling, place the filling ingredients in a large bowl and mix well.
5. Break the pasta dough into lemon-size pieces. Shape each piece into a long, thin sheet. Cut the sheet into small strips 2 inches wide, then into little squares, about 2 inches square. Place ½ teaspoon of filling on each square and shape immediately into a triangle. Seal edges securely,

using a little egg wash if necessary to make it stick. Hold the triangle in your right hand and fold it around your left index finger so that the two ends curl around and overlap each other. Repeat until all squares are done.

6. Spread the tortelloni out to dry on a parchment-lined cookie sheet, making sure they do not touch. Bring a large pot of water to a boil. Add salt and boil the tortellini for 5 to 7 minutes. Drain and place in a serving dish. Toss with Fresh Tomato Sauce and serve.

1 tablespoon chopped fresh Italian parsley

Egg wash made by combining 1 egg yolk and 1 combining tablespoon water

Salsa al Pomodoro

Fresh Tomato Sauce

Makes 3–4 Cups

Sea salt
Fresh Tomato Sauce

Steps and Procedures

1. In a 2-quart pot, blanch the tomatoes in boiling water for a few minutes. Drain, then peel. Discard the seeds, chop, and set aside.

2. In a 4-quart nonreactive saucepan, sauté the onion, carrot, celery, and garlic in the olive oil until the onion is transparent, about 5 minutes.

3. Add the prepared tomatoes and hot pepper. Cook over medium heat for 20 minutes, or until reduced. Add the basil.

4. Season with salt and pepper, and cook for an additional 10 minutes.

5. Store in the refrigerator for 2 days or freeze for up to 3 months.

2 pounds ripe Italian plum tomatoes
1 small onion, finely minced
1 carrot, grated
1 stalk celery, minced
2 cloves garlic, peeled and minced
4 tablespoons extra-virgin olive oil
⅛ teaspoon hot pepper flakes
2 tablespoons chopped fresh basil
2 cups strained tomato sauce
1 teaspoon sea salt
½ teaspoon freshly ground black pepper

Christmas at Nonna Luisa's

My family would gather every Christmas at the home of Nonna Luisa. December 24 was a day of busy preparations. Italian tradition calls for decorating the tree and setting the nativity scene on Christmas Eve. Nonna Luisa had the most elaborate nativity set. While most families celebrate the scene at the manger, Nonna Luisa had an entire village. She had mountains, ponds, and miniature forests. The town bustled with merchants and shepherds and fishermen. The manger sported every animal as well as a chorus of angels. The entire set was displayed on the length of a table. The only figure missing was the baby Jesus, which was placed after returning from Mass. My grandmother and cousins and I would spend the entire day cooking in the kitchen before attending Christmas Eve Mass in downtown Bologna. I loved the excitement of hearing all the church bells around Bologna ring at midnight, heralding Christmas morning.

Christmas Day was a time of family. We'd feast on the rich and colorful dishes. Nonno Tullio would pick a special wine and pour everyone a glass to toast the birth of Christ. There was no Santa Claus in our celebrations. Italian children waited for the Epiphany to receive gifts from a magical person, La Befana. As a child, in school I learned the fallowing story about La Befana. I still remember how excited we would get as the teacher read the story.

The Legend of La Befana

An old woman steadily sweeps her home. As the broom brushes along the wooden floor planks of her cottage, her donkey begins to bray. The woman hobbles to open the door to see three beautifully dressed men pass by her. Covered in gold, velvet, and silk, the men gaze up at the sky searching the eastern horizon.

They slowly headed toward the small rays of rising sun creeping over the darkness. The woman calls out to them. "Fine sirs, where are you traveling with such ornate clothing and gifts?" The men tell her of their quest to follow the North Star, which should lead them to a newborn king. She brings them fruit, nuts, and other sweets for this journey. In turn, they invite her to join them in their pilgrimage, but the woman looks at her aging donkey and frayed broom, and feels humbled by the riches of the Magi, so she refuses and returns to her cottage.

But the woman's donkey continues to bray and she once again steps out of her house to see what is exciting such an old donkey. She becomes filled with the light of the North Star and realizes she does want to see the birth of a new king. So she gathers little toys and fruits and nuts in an old sack as gifts for the little baby and sets off to find him. In some homes it is believed she rides her donkey, in others she rides her broom. But on the eve of the Epiphany she rides over the cities of Italy in search of the newborn king. Every January 6, La Befana, still dressed in her simple black dress and shawl, flies over Italy and down the chimneys to deliver little toys, fruits, and nuts to the children.

If a child is good, the child finds wonderful treats waiting for him or her in the morning. But if a child is naughty, there is a lump of coal waiting in his or her stocking, in hopes the child will burn the coal and find a light that warms the heart as the North Star's brightness filled La Befana's heart. Although she is often depicted as a very old and ugly in tattered clothing, the children of Italy love La Befana like a magical grandmother and sings songs on her honor on the Epiphany. My friends and I would sing the following song:

La Befana vien di notte	La Befana comes at night
con le scarpe tutte rotte	With her shoes all broken
con le toppe alla sottana.	And her outfit patched.
Viva viva la Befana.	Long live la Befana.

La Befana no longer places nuts and fruit in childrens' stockings on the Epiphany but leaves delicious Italian candy

If a child is good, the child finds wonderful treats waiting for him or her in the morning.

and other presents under the tree. Coal is still given but it is made of a sugar-candy licorice. My parents would give me and my sister a piece of coal candy every year saying, "You were naughty at least once." Secretly I liked the coal candy the best.

Since the Epiphany is a big holiday for Italians, my mother would be working from early morning until lunchtime baking and selling last-minute treats for other families' gatherings. She would tell my father to wait before letting me open all my gifts from La Befana until she came home. That was the best and worst part of the celebration, knowing all my gifts waited for me just on the other side of the living room door and not being able to see them until after lunch. However, one holiday my dad fell asleep while waiting for my mother to arrive from work, and I sneaked into the living room. I opened up all my gifts before either of them knew it. Needless to say, the next year I received more than one lump of coal in my stocking.

Lasagne Verdi alla Bolognese
Lasagne Bolognese Style
Serves 8

Enjoy the best lasagne you have ever had, made with thin layers of spinach noodles, topped with Bolognese sauce and a delicate cheese sauce. In Bologna every family has its own interpretation of this classic dish. Light in taste, it has become a favorite with my students. Use the frozen spinach instead of fresh since it will incorporate into the dough much better.

Steps and Procedures

1. Cook the spinach according to the package directions. Drain and purée using a food processor or blender. Set aside and let cool completely.
2. Place flour on a wooden board and form into a mound.
3. Make a deep well in the center and break the eggs, into it. Add salt and cooked spinach. Use a fork to break up the eggs and mix the contents of the well.
4. Slowly add the flour, beginning at the top of the well collapse and blend into the mixture. When flour is almost totally absorbed, begin kneading, pressing with the palms of your hands. Knead dough for about 20 minutes, until it becomes smooth and elastic. (If dough is dry, add a few drops of water. If it is sticky, add a sprinkle of flour.)
5. Gather the dough into a ball, place it in a mixing bowl, cover with plastic wrap, and let rest for 30 minutes. (To test for readiness, punch the dough with your index finger. If it springs back, it is done.)
6. Cut the dough into small strips 2-inches-by-4-inches and spread out to dry.

Pasta

1 package (10 ounces) frozen chopped spinach

4 cups all-purpose unbleached flour

2 large eggs

1 teaspoon sea salt

Ragù Alla Bolognese

1 carrot, peeled and finely minced

1 stalk celery, trimmed and finely minced

1 small yellow onion, peeled and finely minced

2 tablespoons extra-virgin olive oil

½ pound finely diced pancetta (Italian bacon)

2 pounds lean ground veal

(Continued)

1 cup dry red wine
1 can (16 ounces)
   chopped tomatoes
2 cans (16 ounces
   each) tomato
   sauce
1 teaspoon sea salt
¼ teaspoon freshly
   ground black
   pepper

Besciamelle (Béchamel) Sauce

3 cups whole milk
6 tablespoons
   unsalted butter
6 tablespoons all-
   purpose
   unbleached flour
1 teaspoon sea salt
½ teaspoon freshly
   ground white
   pepper
½ cup freshly grated
   Parmigiano
   Reggiano cheese
½ teaspoon freshly
   grated nutmeg
Water and salt, as
   needed to cook
   pasta
1 cup freshly grated
   Parmigiano
   Reggiano cheese

To Prepare the Bolognese Sauce

In a large 8-quart heavy-bottomed, nonreactive stockpot, cook the carrot, celery, and onion in olive oil over medium heat until the onion is transparent. Add the pancetta and veal. Cook until the meats are lightly brown. Add the wine and cook until it evaporates. Add the chopped tomatoes and sauce to the mixture. Season with salt and pepper. Lower the heat and simmer, partly covered, stirring once in a while, for 55 minutes, until sauce thickens. Adjust the seasoning and reserve.

To Prepare the Béchamel Sauce

Heat the milk in a small 2-quart saucepan. In a separate pan, melt the butter and immediately stir in the flour, salt, and pepper. While whisking the mixture, slowly add the hot milk a little at a time. Allow the mixture to thicken over low heat while whisking (about 10 minutes). Remove the pan from the heat and stir in the cheese and nutmeg.

To Assemble

Preheat the oven to 350°F. Bring water to a boil, add salt, then pasta. Boil for 4 to 5 minutes. Drain and place the pasta in a cold-water bath. Drain on cloth towel. Cover the bottom of a deep 9-by-13-inch-by-2 inch baking dish with Bolognese sauce. Add enough lasagna noodle strips to cover the bottom evenly. Spread another layer of Bolognese sauce and then the béchamel sauce. Sprinkle with grated cheese. Add another layer of lasagna noodles, Bolognese sauce, béchamel sauce, and cheese. Add a final layer of noodles. Cover with Bolognese sauce, béchamel sauce, and cheese. Cover with plastic wrap, then top with aluminum foil. Bake in the preheated oven for 45 minutes. Remove baking dish from oven and let set for 10 minutes before cutting and serving.

Galantina alla Galantini
Boneless Stuffed Capon

Serves 12

At Christmastime a capon was always part of our meal. At the market my grandmother would buy the biggest one she could find. She would then bring it home and wash it thoroughly, then bone and stuff it. She would use the bones to make the stock. On Christmas Day the capon would be roasted not boiled and the tortellini would be cooked in the broth. I made this recipe for my very first dinner party as a young bride. I had the butcher bone the capon for me and I received great reviews from all my guests. Buy a farm-raised capon from a reputable source and have it boned. Capons have an incomparable flavor and texture and are worth the extra trouble of finding them and paying the cost.

Steps and Procedures

1. Wash the capon, remove the giblets, and wipe the bird inside and out.
2. Starting from the neck area, begin undressing the capon from its neck down its back. Make a long cut down the spine; open the capon as you would a book; take as much meat off the bones as you can.
3. Taking care not to damage the skin, cut through the leg and wing joints, cutting off the upper thigh bones and removing the meat from the breastbone. Remove all bones and any cartilage. Preheat the oven at 400°F.
4. Season the boneless capon with ½ cup of wine, and the salt and pepper. Cover with plastic wrap and refrigerate until ready. Save the bones for preparing the stock.
5. In a 10-inch sauté pan, melt the butter, then add the onion and celery.
6. Cook until soft. Cool slightly and place into a stainless-

A 3-to-4-pound whole capon
1 cup dry white wine
1 teaspoon sea salt
1 teaspoon freshly ground black pepper
4 tablespoons unsalted butter
1 large onion, peeled and finely chopped
2 stocks celery, finely chopped
2 cups fresh bread crumbs
2 large eggs
½ cup grated Parmigiano Reggiano cheese
¼ cup finely chopped fresh Italian parsley
½ teaspoon fresh thyme leaves
Additional sea salt and black pepper to taste

(Continued)

La Cucina della Nonna Luisa

45

⅛ teaspoon freshly
    grated nutmeg
1 cup capon stock
8 thin slices prosciutto
    di Parma
1 teaspoon extra-
    virgin olive oil

Sauce

1 shallot, peeled and
    finely minced
4 tablespoons
    unsalted butter
1 tablespoon porcini
    mushrooms
    soaked in stock
¼ cup dry white wine
2 cups capon stock
1 teaspoon sea salt
½ teaspoon freshly
    grated white
    pepper
1 cup heavy whipping
    cream

steel mixing bowl. Add the bread crumbs, eggs, grated cheese, parsley, thyme, salt, pepper, and nutmeg and mix well. Keep the mixture moist with 1 cup of the prepared stock.

7. Cover the inside of the capon with prosciutto slices, then top with dressing.

8. Sew up the capon with kitchen twine, giving it its original shape, then truss with butcher string and place in parchment paper brushed with olive oil. Season with salt and pepper. Drizzle the capon with some of the prepared stock and the remaining wine, then seal the parchment paper like a package; place the capon in a large baking dish.

9. Roast the capon in the preheated oven for 1½ hours, or until the temperature in the thickest part of the capon reaches 170°F. on an-instant-read thermometer. Baste frequently during cooking time. Remove the paper and let the capon brown during the last 15 minutes of the cooking process. Remove the bird from the oven and let it cool at room temperature.

10. To prepare the sauce, cook the shallot in butter in a 2-quart saucepan set over high heat. Add the porcini mushrooms and reserve the broth. Add the wine and reduce for 5 minutes over high heat.

11. Add the stock and porcini juice. Reduce by half. Temper the cream in the sauce and season with salt and pepper. Cook over high heat until the sauce starts to thicken and coats the back of a spoon.

12. Slice the capon and serve with the prepared sauce.

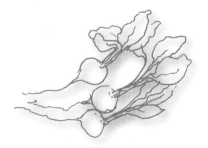

Zuppa Inglese
English Trifle
Serves 8

The origin of the name of this dessert is quite a mystery. Zuppa Inglese translates as "English Soup." It is very popular in Bologna, with every family having their own version. My Nonna Louisa made hers with Alkermes, a sweet red-colored liqueur, but fruit juice can be substituted. Make it the day before and the liquor will flavor the cake.

Steps and Procedures

1. Preheat the oven to 350°F. Butter and flour a 13-by-18-inch jelly-roll pan.
2. Beat the egg whites with the salt in an electric mixer until stiff peaks form.
3. Beat the egg yolks with the sugar, butter, lemon on zest, and vanilla until pale yellow and ribbons form.
4. Sift the flour. Fold the egg whites into the egg yolks one third at a time, alternating with the flour.
5. Pour the batter into the prepared pan. Bake for 25 to 30 minutes.
6. Remove the sponge cake from the oven and set it aside to cool.
7. To make the custard, heat the milk in a 1-quart saucepan. In a bowl, mix the egg yolks, vanilla, cornstarch, and sugar.
8. Add the milk to the mixture a little at a time.
9. Return saucepan to the stove and stir constantly until mixture thickens and coats the back of a spoon. Cover with plastic wrap and refrigerate to chill.
10. To make the syrup bring the water and sugar to a boil in

Pan di Spagna Sponge
Butter and flour for preparing pan
8 large eggs, separated
Pinch salt
1 cup granulated sugar
¼ cup melted unsalted butter
1 teaspoon lemon zest
1 teaspoon vanilla sugar or extract
1½ cup all-purpose flour

Custard
2 cups whole milk
4 large egg yolks
1 teaspoon vanilla extract
3 tablespoons all-purpose cornstarch
½ cup granulated sugar

Chocolate
Custard

*The same ingredients
as for a regular
custard but add 2
tablespoons
unsweetened cocoa
or 3 ounces melted
semisweet
chocolate*

Syrup

*1 cup water
1 cup granulated
sugar
¼ cup Sloe Gin*

1-quart saucepan. Boil until the sugar is dissolved—about 10 minutes. Cool and mix with Sloe Gin.

11. To assemble the trifle, cut the cake into ½-inch slices width-wise. Brush 1 side of the slices with the syrup.

12. In a decorative glass bowl, layer one third of the cake soaked-side down. Sprinkle with syrup. Spread custard over it. Place the second cake layer of cake in the bowl. Brush both sides with syrup and spread custard over it.

13. Refrigerate until ready to serve.

Croccante

Hazelnut Brittle

Serves 10–12

A fun, easy recipe that will please old and young alike. During the holiday season, under the porticos of one of the oldest churches in Bologna, Chiesa dei Servi, vendors would set up their goods and sell toys, candy, and holiday decorations, including nativity figures. My Nonna would take us there to buy our favorite candy and a figurine each for our nativity set. Croccante would always be my choice. Buy nuts from a reputable source and keep them in the freezer until ready to use. To make the croccante, I use an iron skillet. Be very careful not to burn yourself with the hot sugar.*

8 ounces hazelnuts
8 ounces almonds
2 tablespoons
    unsalted butter
    plus extra for
    greasing cookie
    sheet
1 lemon
2 cups granulated
    sugar

Steps and Procedures

1. Prepare the nuts. Toast the hazelnuts on a 10-inch skillet on top of the stove until light golden in color. Place nuts in a clean kitchen towel and rub the skins off. Remove and coarsely chop. Boil the almonds for 10 minutes to loosen the skins, then drain and peel, toast in the hot skillet until lightly golden in color. Remove and coarsely chop.

2. Line a cookie sheet or marble slab with aluminum foil. Butter it and reserve. Cut the lemon in half.

3. Melt the sugar and the juice of ½ lemon over low heat in a 12-inch heavy copper or iron skillet, until light gold in color. Sugar will caramelize at 320°F. on a candy thermometer. Do not burn the sugar.

4. Stir in the prepared nuts; continue stirring until the nuts are completely coated with sugar. Stir in the 2 tablespoons butter.

5. Turn off the heat. Working quickly, pour the mixture onto the prepared sheet.
6. With the other ½ lemon, flatten and smooth the sugar mixture, being careful not to get burned. This will cool the mixture quickly, preventing it from getting darker.
7. Cool brittle completely and crack to serve.

"Smoked" Polenta

Steaming hot and deliciously filling, polenta has been a staple for families in Northern Italy for more than five hundred years. These days, the regions of Lombardy and Veneto still fight for polenta supremacy. Maize arrived in Europe with Christopher Columbus's discovery of the New World. The Incas, Aztecs, and Mayas had successfully grown the grain and had built their civilizations on it. The Spanish conquistadors realized the richness of maize and the golden grains soon multiplied in the fertile soil of Europe.

The first recipe for grain mush, or "puls," came from astronomer Apicius, in his famous manuscript, the world's first cookbook. Later the Romans in the first century made the dish out of a mush using millet spelt or chickpea flour. The same recipe and technique is popular today. The only thing that has changed is the grain (white and black has joined gold) and the variations (soft or firm, with sauce or plain).

The art of making polenta is, for many, a ritual. Certain utensils are a must: a deep copper pot called a *paiolo*, a long, flat wooden spoon, plus two strong arms and lots of patience. The precise combination of flour and water, along with the long, constant cooking process, helps the starch escape from the hard core of the grain, making the polenta lighter and easier to digest.

In my family, my dad's mom, Nonna Luisa, was the polenta expert. During the winter months, we would gather at her house for a *polentata*—a delicious meal of polenta accompanied by much laughter. We would sit around her long table, just waiting for the polenta to finish cooking. My grandmother always said, "You can wait for the polenta, but the polenta can't wait for you."

Nonna Louisa's secret to good polenta was to wait until she thought the polenta was done (about 50-minutes of cooking), then add a little more water to the pan, and stir in the same direction for 15-minutes. Only then would she say the polenta was done. Her polenta always was light and smooth. She would pour the polenta onto a wooden board, which was placed at the center of her long table, then smooth it out, and, with the help of a string held between her hands, cut it into slices while still warm. My grandmother always had a special sauce and lots of cheese for the top. Rabbit, sausage, mushroom, or bean stews were her favorite sauces.

The most memorable *polentata* took place on a cold winter day. My grandmother liked to keep warm by using a common warming device called *il prete*, or "priest." It looked like a wooden snake that had just swallowed dinner. You would plug the priest in and slip it under the covers of your bed to warm the sheets before you went to bed.

That evening we had gathered at her house for our weekly *polentata* and were spreading the golden mass out on the table, the stew was bubbling on the stove, and our mouths were watering in anticipation when a strange burning smell drifted out of Nonna's bedroom and mixed in the air with the sweet aroma of the polenta. It was not until the smoke began to billow out of Nonna's bedroom that we realized her bed had caught on fire. My family attempted to get in the bedroom to unplug and remove the priest but it had already started to smolder. So we evacuated the house while someone called the fire department. Nonna was distraught but not over her bedroom so much as her beautiful polenta. The firemen sprinted up the stairs to my Nonna's place and were able to contain the fire to her bed with little damage to her room and the rest of the building. And, most importantly to my Nonna, they saved dinner. To show her gratitude she invited the entire fire department back to her kitchen to share in our *polentata*.

The art of

making polenta

is, for many,

a ritual.

Polenta ai Funghi

Polenta with Mushroom Sauce

Serves 8

This polenta dish is great because it can be made ahead of time. It is important to make a thick polenta. My special way to serve polenta is to take the hardened leftover pieces, brush them with olive oil and grill them for a few minutes, then remove them from the broiler and top with cheese. It is wonderful! The only problem? In my family, there's rarely any leftover polenta.

Steps and Procedures

1. To make the polenta, heat the water in a deep pot. Add the salt and butter. Slowly, in a steady stream, add the cornmeal while constantly whisking. Reduce the heat to low, being very careful not to let the mixture burn.
2. Switch to a wooden spoon and continue to stir until the polenta mixture comes away from the sides of the pot. Usually it takes 40 minutes to cook.
3. Pour the cooked polenta onto a wet marble slab. Smooth the polenta with a spatula (dip frequently in hot water to prevent stickiness) to 1-inch thickness. Cover with foil and reserve.
4. Slice polenta with a piece of string. Place slices on an oiled baking dish and cover with sauce (recipe procedures follow). Sprinkle with cheese.
5. Bake at 350°F. for 30 minutes. Serve immediately.
6. To prepare the tomato sauce, blanch the tomatoes in boiling water for a few minutes. Drain and peel, then chop and reserve.
7. Cook the sausage, drain off the fat and reserve.

Classic Polenta
4 cups water
1 teaspoon sea salt
2 tablespoons butter
1 cup fine cornmeal
1 cup course cornmeal

Grated Parmigiano
   Reggiano cheese
   for topping

Fresh Tomato Sauce
1 pound ripe tomatoes
½ pound bulk Italian
   sausage
1 onion, peeled and
   finely chopped
2 cloves garlic, peeled
   and minced
1 carrot, peeled and
   grated
2 ounces soaked
   porcini mushrooms
½ pound mushrooms,
   washed and sliced

(Continued)

*4 tablespoons extra-
  virgin olive oil*
¼ cup dry white wine
*⅛ teaspoon hot red
  pepper flakes*
2 cups tomato sauce
*1 tablespoon chopped
  freshly Italian
  parsley*
1 teaspoon sea salt
*1 teaspoon freshly
  ground pepper*

8. In a large skillet, sauté the onion, garlic, carrot, drained porcini mushrooms, and other mushrooms in the oil until the onion is transparent.
9. Add cooked the sausage. Pour in the wine and cook until it evaporates.
10. Add the prepared tomatoes and hot pepper flakes. Cook over medium heat for ten minutes.
11. Add the tomato sauce and cook for 20 minutes.
12. Chop the parsley and add to the sauce. Season with salt and pepper. Cook for another 10 minutes. Reserve.

Osso Buco

Braised Veal Shanks

Serves 6

A perfect dish for supper on a cold winter night. Traditionally a Milanese dish served with risotto, in Bologna it is served with polenta. Choose 2-inch thick slices of veal shank and marinate them in wine overnight. Slowly simmer for 2 to 3 hours until the meat falls off the bone and serve with gremolata sauce. Make sure to try the bone marrow, which is considered the best part of the dish. In Bologna a waiter will very politely ask you if there was something wrong with the dish if you sent it back to the kitchen with the marrow untouched.

Steps and Procedures

1. Marinate the veal shanks in the wine for at least 2 hours, but preferably overnight, in the refrigerator. Season the veal shanks with pepper. Coat with flour and lightly brown on all sides in the oil and butter in a 12-inch sauté pan. Remove from the pan and reserve.

2. Add the onion, carrot, and celery to the pan. Cook over medium heat until slightly wilted.

6 veal shanks
  (6 ounces each)
1 cup dry white wine
½ teaspoon freshly
  ground black pepper
2 tablespoons all-
  purpose flour
¼ cup extra-virgin
  olive oil
2 tablespoons
  unsalted butter
1 small onion peeled
  and finely minced
1 carrot, peeled and
  finely minced
1 stalk celery,
  trimmed and
  finely minced
1 pound ripe Roma
  tomatoes, peeled,
  seeded, and chopped
1 cup tomato sauce
1 teaspoon sea salt

(Continued)

*2 cups defatted veal
stock (or beef stock
if veal not available)*

Gremolata
Sauce

*1 tablespoon chopped
fresh Italian
parsley
2 cloves garlic, peeled
and minced
1 tablespoon lemon
zest*

3. Add the fresh tomatoes and tomato sauce. Sprinkle with salt.
4. Place the prepared veal back in the pan. Cook, partly covered, at a simmer for 2 to 3 hours.
5. During the cooking add stock as needed and braise until the meat is tender.
6. To make the gremolata, in a small bowl mix together the parsley, garlic, and lemon zest. Sprinkle on top of the veal before serving.

Salsiccia e Fagioli
Sausage and Beans
Serves 8

Emilia Romagna is the region of Italy where pork products are king: prosciutto, mortadella, salami, zampone, cotechino, culatello are just a few of its superstars. My grandfather made sausage in the fall and would hang it up to dry for several hours. In order to have a good flavor, sausage must be 40 percent fat. Cook a little patty and taste for seasoning. This dish is appealing to the eye, easy to prepare, can be made ahead, can be frozen, and is delicious!

Steps and Procedures

1. Soak the beans overnight in cold water. Drain and rinse. In a 6-quart stockpot bring the stock and chopped tomatoes to a boil. Add the prepared beans and simmer for 2 to 3 hours.

2. Prepare the sausage by cutting the three meats into 1-inch pieces. Grind the pork, pancetta, and fat together through a meat grinder twice. Do not use the food processor. Preheat heat the oven to 350°F.

3. In a large bowl, mix the meats with the garlic, parsley, cheese, salt, pepper, crushed red pepper and wine. Stuff mixture into casings and tie with butcher strings into 4-inch links. With a sharp needle, prick sausage all over. Hang to dry for one hour.

Homemade Sausage

3 pounds pork butt
½ pound pancetta
½ pound pork fat
3 cloves garlic peeled and minced
1 tablespoon chopped freshly Italian parsley
¼ cup grated Parmigiano Reggiano cheese
2 teaspoons sea salt
1 teaspoon freshly ground pepper
½ teaspoon crushed red pepper flakes
¼ cup dry white wine
Sausage casings

See page 58 for
Beans Ingredients

Beans

2 cups dried
  cannellini beans
8 cups vegetable stock
2 cups chopped
  tomatoes
1 small onion, peeled
  and chopped
2 cloves garlic, peeled
  and minced
¼ cup extra-virgin
  olive oil
1 teaspoon crushed
  red pepper flakes
¼ cup dry white wine
1 teaspoon sea salt
½ teaspoon freshly
  ground black
  pepper
1 teaspoon chopped
  freshly chopped
  Italian parsley

4. Place the sausages teaspoon crushed red pepper flakes, peeled and minced garlic, ¼ cup of extra-virgin olive oil, and the onion in a 12-inch frying pan and brown on all sides. Add the wine and cook until it evaporates.

5. Add the sausage to the beans. Season with salt and pepper, sprinkle with chopped parsley, and cook for another 20 minutes at a simmer. Serve on top of polenta garnished with a sprinkle of cheese.

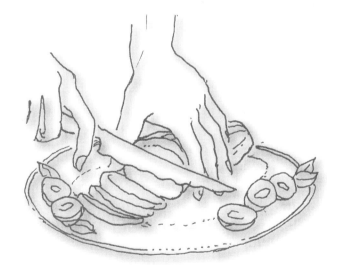

Pollo della Nonna

Grandmother's Chicken

Serves 8

When buying chicken I always tell my students to look for the largest chicken with the biggest breast, but look for a nice plump one, naturally grown, fresh not frozen. Today to find a good chicken is quite a task, but the taste will be worth all the effort.

Steps and Procedures:

1. Season the chicken with salt and pepper. Heat the oil in a large sauté pan and brown the chicken well on all sides.
2. Stir in the prosciutto and cook for 5 minutes. Add the garlic and onion. When the onion becomes transparent, stir in the tomatoes, raise the heat, and cook, stirring until the tomato juices begin to evaporate. Add the tomato sauce and stock.
3. Simmer the chicken for 40 minutes. Add the vinegar; cook for another 10 minutes. Taste and adjust seasonings.
4. Remove the chicken to a serving platter and pour the sauce over the bird and sprinkle with parsley.

A 3-pound chicken, cut into 8 pieces
1 teaspoon sea salt
1 teaspoon freshly ground black pepper
2 tablespoons extra-virgin olive oil
¼ pound prosciutto di Parma, chopped into small cubes
4 cloves garlic, peeled and minced
1 small onion, peeled and chopped
1 pound ripe Roma tomatoes, seeded and chopped
1 cup tomato sauce
1 cup chicken stock
2 tablespoons balsamic vinegar
1 teaspoon chopped fresh Italian parsley

Peperonata

Spicy Pepper Salad

Serves 8

¼ cup extra-virgin
   olive oil
2 onions, peeled and
   sliced
½ teaspoon crushed
   red pepper flakes
2 pounds red and
   yellow peppers,
   cored and cut into
   wide slices
1 pound ripe Roma
   tomatoes, seeded
   and chopped
1 teaspoon sea salt
⅛ teaspoon freshly
   ground black
   pepper
1 cup tomato sauce
1 teaspoon chopped
   fresh basil

My grandmother used to make this side dish all the time. The aroma would fill the house. My cousins and I used to get into so much trouble for going into the kitchen with a piece of bread and dunking it in the steaming mixture. It is a spicy hot salad that can be tossed with pasta, rice, or served on top of polenta.

Steps and Procedures
1.   In a large 12-inch sauté pan, heat the oil and add the onion, then cook until soft.
2.   Add the crushed pepper and red and yellow peppers and cook for 5 minutes over high heat.
3.   Add the tomatoes, pepper, and salt, cook for 5 minutes, then add the tomato sauce. Lower the heat and cook for another 20 minutes.
4.   Sprinkle with basil and taste for seasoning.
5.   Place on a platter and serve.

Summer in the Country

In the summer visiting my aunt's home in the country was always an adventure. My grandmother, my cousins, and I would go on expeditions in the forests surrounding the mountain to forage for mushrooms. The best time to find mushrooms is immediately after a rain. We'd put on our boots and carry a large wicker basket each as we tromped to the woods in search of mushroom clusters. Italy's rich forest climate is ideal for wild mushrooms. There are so many varieties. Nonna, my aunt Paola, my cousin Germana, and I would walk slowly around the trees, going as far as we could away from the path and into the heart of the forest. The green moss and damp bark filled the forest air with a wet sweetness that cooled your face as the sun peeped through the tree canopies and warmed your cheeks. We giggled in delight at every mushroom we found, as each was a treasure to us.

On occasion we'd dine out while in the country. My favorite restaurant experiences revolve around one of Bologna's treasures—La Sfoglina. A *sfoglina* is a woman whose sole occupation is making pasta for restaurants. The sfoglina start working in restaurants at fifteen. Having devoted their lives to making pasta, they develop a phenomenal skill. The *sfoglina* use only the freshest eggs, which have red-tinted yolks. These eggs turn the pasta dough the same deep yellow hue as a sunflower. The dough is rolled out with a special rolling pin. The pin has only one handle and is smooth on the other end. It is said a good *sfoglina* is worth her rolling pin's weight in gold. You can tell an expert *sfoglina* by the size of her rolling pin—the larger the rolling pin the more dough a *sfoglina* is able to work at one time. When rolled out the dough becomes almost transparent. The sfoglina cut and shape the dough into the desired pasta. *Sfoglina* have mammoth arms from working the dough all day. They take great pride in their pasta and often it is the pasta cre-

The *sfoglina*

would make

quick work of

turning her

dough into

pasta.

ated by the *sfoglina* that determines the success of a restaurant.

The restaurant my family would visit in the country had a work area for the *sfoglina* in the front window. She would make pasta as the patrons watched. A close friend of my grandmother, the *sfoglina* would invite me to assist her in making pasta. As a special trick, the *sfoglina* would add white wine to her pasta mixture. This would remove the raw egg flavor and help the dough stay light. Then she would show me how to knead with the palms of my hands while using my arm muscles and we'd knead the dough together.

Eventually she'd cut a small piece for me to roll out and shape into pasta. The *sfoglina* would make quick work of turning her dough into pasta. I would watch her powerful hands cut and shape each piece and then I would try to mimic her techniques. With almost three hundred and fifty different shapes of pasta in her repertoire, that wasn't always an easy task. She would always place my pasta to one side to allow me to take mine home with me. I once asked her why she didn't include my pasta with the ones that were going to the chef to be prepared for the restaurant. She smiled and answered that my pasta was too good and she was afraid if people tasted my pasta that they would not want to eat hers anymore. As a child I truly believed I must have magical pasta powers if I could make pasta that rivaled that of a great *sfoglina*. This belief sealed my passion for cooking.

As wisdom comes with age so does techniques for pasta making, and while I might have a little pasta-making magic I don't think anyone could rival the *sfoglina's* pasta or her kindness.

La Ieda

Pasta with Walnut Sauce

Serves 6

The love affair that Italians have with pasta spread across the Atlantic at the turn of the century with the arrival of immigrants. Pasta is a quick and frugal dish that can be made in no time and gets rave reviews every time it is served. This sauce is made traditionally in Italy for "Ferragosto," the fifteenth of August, when all the grocery stores in Italy are closed for a national vacation, since the dish requires ingredients normally found in every home.

Steps and Procedures

1. Bring an 8-quart pot of water to boil. Add salt, then pasta, and cook until the penne are *al dente*, 7 to 8 minutes. Drain and set aside.
2. In a 2-quart saucepan, boil the walnuts a few at a time for 5 to 6 minutes. Remove and skin the nuts.
3. Put the prepared walnuts and the bread crumbs in the food processor or blender and process until a fine texture is achieved. Add milk as needed to create a pastelike consistency.
4. Heat the oil and butter in a 12-inch frying pan. Add the garlic and red pepper flaked. Cook over high heat for 2 to 3 minutes. Add the walnut mixture and cook for another 5 minutes.
5. Season the pasta with salt and pepper and chopped parsley.
6. In a large bowl toss the sauce with the prepared pasta. Sprinkle the grated cheese on top and serve immediately.

Salt for seasoning pasta cooking water

1 pound dry penne pasta

1 pound fresh shelled walnuts

½ cup fresh bread crumbs

¼ cup whole milk

¼ cup extra-virgin olive oil

2 tablespoons unsalted butter

4 cloves garlic, peeled and minced

⅛ teaspoon crushed red pepper flakes

1 teaspoon sea salt

½ teaspoon freshly ground black pepper

1 teaspoon chopped fresh Italian parsley

2 tablespoons fresh grated Parmigiano Reggiano cheese

Frittata di Erbette

Herb Omelet

Serves 8

¼ cup extra-virgin
olive oil
1 onion, peeled and
coarsely chopped
2 cloves garlic, peeled
and minced
2 zucchini, coarsely
chopped
2 sweet red peppers,
coarsely chopped
12 large eggs
½ cup grated
Parmigiano
Reggiano cheese
1 tablespoon whole milk
½ teaspoon fresh thyme
1 teaspoon fresh basil,
rolled up and
chopped into strips
(chiffonaded)
1 teaspoon minced
fresh Italian
parsley
1 teaspoon sea salt
1 teaspoon freshly
ground black pepper

In the summertime, in the country, my Nonna would make a light supper by serving us a frittata with a big salad. In the morning she would pick a variety of herbs and a few vegetables from the garden. Then we would be awakened by the chickens as she went to their shed to collect the fresh eggs and we would say to each other, "Nonna is making a frittata."

Steps and Procedures

1. Heat the oil in a heavy 12-inch ovenproof nonstick skillet. Add the onion, garlic, zucchini, and peppers. Cook until the onion becomes golden in color over medium heat. Preheat the oven to 400°F.
2. In a small bowl, whisk the eggs with half the cheese (¼ cup) and the milk, herbs, salt, and pepper.
3. Add the egg mixture to the sautéed vegetables and cook over low heat until the bottom is set and tiny bubbles form on the top. Remove the skillet from the stove.
4. Place the skillet in the oven to finish baking, about 10 minutes or until the top is set. Sprinkle with the remaining cheese and let it cool before serving.

Arrosto di Maiale alle Albicocche

Apricot-Stuffed Roast Pork Loin

Serves 8

Pork is very popular in Bologna since is so readily available. Center-cut loin or tenderloin are my favorite choices. I remember that several years ago I could not offer a class that had pork as the main course, but today pork is as popular here as it is in Italy. I like to cook my roast until well done (160° to 170°F. on an instant-read thermometer). This recipe can be made with fresh apricots, plums, or peaches or, when not in season, you can substitute dry fruit.

Steps and Procedures:

1. Using a knife, butterfly the pork loin, making a lengthwise cut down the center of the pork, cutting three-quarters of the way through. Open as you would a book. Place the pork in a glass baking dish.

2. Sprinkle on the vinegar, oil, garlic, rosemary, and 1 teaspoon of the black pepper. Cover with plastic wrap, and place the dish in the refrigerator to marinate overnight.

3. Combine the apricots and liqueur in a small bowl. Macerate for 30 minutes. Drain the apricots, reserving the liqueur. Chop the fruit and mix with the chives.

4. Preheat the oven to 450°F. Remove the pork from the marinade and pat dry, discarding the marinade.

5. Spread the apricot mixture in center of the pork. Bring the halves together and tie with butcher string. Transfer the pork to 13-by-9-by-2-inch stainless-steel baking pan. Brush with 1 tablespoon of the jam.

6. Roast the pork until it begins to brown, about 20 minutes. Reduce oven temperature to 350°F. Season with salt and

3-pound boneless pork loin (center cut)

¼ cup white wine vinegar

4 tablespoons extra-virgin olive oil

3 garlic cloves, peeled and minced

1 teaspoon fresh rosemary, finely chopped

2 teaspoons freshly ground pepper

12 large pitted fresh or dry apricots

½ cup Triple Sec liqueur

1 teaspoon fresh chopped chives

2 tablespoons apricot jam

1 teaspoon sea salt

½ cup defatted chicken stock

1 cup heavy whipping cream

Salt and pepper for seasoning

the remaining teaspoon of pepper. Continue roasting until a thermometer inserted into thickest part of pork registers 170°F. (about 40 minutes). Transfer roast to a platter, then tent with foil.

7. Deglaze the roasting pan with the reserved liqueur, scraping off the bottom of the baking pan any browned bits. Transfer the essence to a 2-quart saucepan and then add stock and the cream. Set the saucepan over high heat; bring to a boil and cook until the sauce thickens Later about 10 to 15 minutes). Season with salt and pepper to taste. Strain the sauce and reserve. Remove the string from the pork roast. Slice the pork and serve it with the sauce.

Pollo ai Funghi Porcini

Chicken Breasts with Porcini Mushroom Sauce

Serves 8

A quick and easy dish to prepare, my Nonna would use chicken, turkey, or veal—and, of course, fresh porcini mushrooms—to prepare this classic.

Steps and Procedures

1. Heat the oil in a 12-inch sauté pan. Add the chopped porcini, reserving the soaking liquid; next add the porto-bellos and garlic.
2. Cut the chicken breasts in half. Pound the chicken breasts with a flat meat mallet to make them even. Coat with sea-soned flour. Add the chicken to the sauté pan and lightly brown on both sides.
3. Add the wine and porcini liquid and cook for 10 minutes.
4. Temper in the cream and cook until the sauce thickens (about 10 minutes).
5. Sprinkle with parsley, nutmeg, salt, and pepper. Serve with mashed potatoes.

4 tablespoons extra-virgin olive oil

¼ cup dried porcini mushrooms, soaked in water

1 cup cleaned and sliced baby portobello mushrooms

4 cloves garlic, peeled and finely chopped

4 whole boneless and skinless chicken breasts

¼ cup all-purpose flour, seasoned with salt and pepper

½ cup dry Marsala wine

1 cup heavy whipping cream

1 teaspoon chopped fresh Italian parsley

⅛ teaspoon freshly grated nutmeg

1 teaspoon sea salt

½ teaspoon freshly ground white pepper

Zuccherini Montanari

Wedding Cookies

Makes 36

4 cups all-purpose
   flour
½ cup powder sugar
1 teaspoon baking
   powder
6 large eggs
½ cup vegetable oil
2 teaspoons fennel
   seeds
2 teaspoons vanilla
   sugar

Glaze:

1 cup powdered sugar
1–2 tablespoons milk
   or lemon juice

Weddings are always a special occasion in Italy, especially in the country-side. The whole town takes part in the celebration. These cookies, shaped like wedding rings, are given to the guests as a token of good wishes. White baskets are decorated with fresh flowers and lined with white cloth. The baskets are then filled with zuccherini and served out-side the church.

Steps and Procedures:

1. Sift together the flour, the powdered sugar, and the baking powder onto a large cutting board. Shape it into the form of a large well. Add the eggs, oil, fennel seeds, and vanilla sugar.
2. Incorporate all ingredients together to form a dough; do not overwork. Place in an oiled bowl, cover with plastic wrap, and let the dough rest for 30 minutes.
3. Preheat oven to 350°F. Cut dough into walnut size pieces and roll out each one into a long rope of medium thickness. Flatten the rope and fold in half-lengths ways. Shape each one into a ring. Pinch the ends together.
4. Place cookies onto a well greased and floured, or parch-ment lined, baking sheet. Bake for 15–20 minutes until lightly golden.
5. Prepare frosting by mixing together sugar and milk.
6. Brush each cookie with glaze while the cookies are still warm.

Life, Love, and Family

Nonna Luisa had made the traditional Sunday dinner. The entire family gathered around the large marble table. A crisp white linen tablecloth anchored down with dusty bottles of wine, carafes of water, and tiny loaves of fresh bread scattered about were commonplace. There were no place settings at grandmother's table, yet every one had their own seat. I chose to sit near my cousins. My grandmother would gather everyone around the table and we'd murmur like a theater crowd when the warning light flashes signaling the start of the performance. Grandmother would enter the room with enormous platters of food. Then Grandfather would enter and walk slowly down the length of the table and sit at his rightful place at the head. Grandfather was always served first, in our family an unspoken tradition, and no one ate until Grandfather took his first bite. My cousins and I made a game out of this, readying our forks to compete to be the first to get a bite in after Grandfather.

But on this night Grandfather was already seated at the table. A heavy cloud of emotion hung over him like a mourning veil. He sat hunched over, staring down toward the end of the table at some unseen guests. Grandma served the children first and the adults were quiet. My cousin laughed when I tickled her, and that brought a disciplinary look from more than just our mothers. Grandfather cleared his throat.

"I received a letter today from the government. They have been requested to send the officer home, he is ill. I have been asked to testify against his release." He spoke slowly, his words thick with tears that would not fall. I looked to my mother for a clue about how to react to this enigmatic statement. My mother sat very still, as did all the adults, suspecting more was going to be said. Grandfather continued to tell the story my cousins and I had previously only heard in snippets of whispered conversations. Something happened to that family—a secret that the adults would either whisper about or in the presence of Great-grandfather avoid altogether, until the past joined us for dinner that evening.

It was during the war. The entire village of Marzabotto was empty of eligible men. They had been drafted from both sides of the fight and sent away. My grandfather had left behind his wife and five children. He had received only one letter from his wife during this time—a telegram informing him she was pregnant with their sixth child. A soldier in the army, he had been captured during battle and sent to a concentration camp in Germany. Tullio spend the days thinking of his family, and imagining the tiny life growing inside his wife. Then word came the fighting had shifted north. Tullio desperately tried to get word to his wife to escape but was persuaded that it was impossible. His companions assured him that the fighting was far from Marzabotto, but that even if the enemy entered the town, there were only women and children, hardly a threat to the Nazis. He was assured that his family needed him alive, what with six children, and to attempt escape would be signing his death certificate. He stayed and spent his days talking to anyone who had information about the fighting in northern Italy.

It was early morning when word came of a terrible massacre in a tiny northern village. The entire population had been herded into the town's church. Those that could not fit in were shot. The women sent the children in first and squeezed as many people in as they could. Then the Nazis demanded information. During their retreat north, the Nazis were attempting to search out freedom fighters who had been finding cover in small villages. One by one the women were led to the Nazis, and when a woman could not—or would not—answer the questions, she was shot. The schoolteacher tried to calm the children and distract them from the gruesome sight before them. The children began to cry as their mothers were killed. The Nazis grew restless from the noise and began firing machine guns into the crowds of children. They ran around the fallen bodies, stabbing at random and seeking out any movement to still those still alive. The Nazis then gathered their forces and continued the march north. The only survivor to give witness to the event was the schoolteacher who had received the first bullets and fell to the ground. Her body was then buried under the children's bodies and she went unnoticed as the Nazis sought out and killed anyone still breathing. The village was Marzabotto. Tullio's wife and children had all been killed.

The officer who gave the orders to wipe out the village had since been captured and had been serving a life sentence in a Roman prison. The letter my grandfather spoke of was about the possible release of this officer. My grandfather went through many years of mourning over his great loss. He felt extreme guilt for not trying to escape and get to his family. It was not until many years later that he fell in love with my grandmother and began to feel any emotion in his numbed heart. It was his new family that sat before him that evening, hanging silently on his every word. He crumpled the letter in his fist. This was the first and last time I would see my grandfather weep.

No one moved. Then my cousin Germana slipped down under the table to escape the confines of her chair, crawled out from under the table, and slowly approached the huddled mass heaving with tears at the head of our table. She slipped her hand in his and said, *"Non piangere Nonno, ci siamo' noi."* "Don't cry, Grandpa, you have us."

With that Grandfather swept my cousin off her feet and hugged her tightly. He turned his eyes to the table before him, and thanked God for giving him a second chance. He went to each person at the table, and held their face in his hands as he smiled, kissed them, and told each one how much he loved them. The ghosts had left. They no longer clung in the air, but seemed to find a restful peace within the hearts of our family. Soon everyone was hugging and crying. We sat down to a meal of very cold pasta and meat. And yet each bite was a sort of blessing, a reaffirmation of life and love and family.

And yet each bite was a sort of blessing, a reaffirmation of life and love and family.

La Cucina della Nonna Luisa

71

Tagliatelle al Prosciutto

Pasta with Prosciutto Sauce

Serves 6

Salt for seasoning
    pasta cooking water
1 pound fresh
    tagliatelle pasta
2 tablespoons extra-
    virgin olive oil
¼ pound prosciutto di
    Parma, cut into
    small cubes
1 small onion, peeled
    and finely minced
1 stalk celery, finely
    minced
1 carrot, peeled and
    finely minced
½ cup dry white wine
2 pounds ripe Roma
    tomatoes, peeled,
    seeded, and chopped
2 tablespoons tomato
    paste
½ teaspoon freshly
    ground pepper
½ teaspoon sea salt
1 tablespoon peas or
    asparagus tips
¼ cup grated
    Parmigiano
    Reggiano cheese

Tagliatelle, 9 millimeters wide, is a type of fettuccine that was created, according to a Bolognese legend, for the wedding of Lucrezia Borgia to immortalize the golden hair of the bride.

Steps and Procedures
1. Bring an 8-quart pot of water to a boil. Add salt, then pasta, and cook until the tagliatelle are *al dente*. Drain pasta.
2. In a 12-inch sauté pan, heat the oil and add the prosciutto, onion, celery, and carrot. Cook over high heat for 10 minutes.
3. Add the wine and let it reduce for 5 minutes. Add the fresh tomatoes, letting them cook for 20 minutes over medium heat. Stir in the tomato paste. Season with pepper and salt (only if needed, depending on the quality of the prosciutto).
4. Cook for another 20 minutes, or until the sauce thickens. Add the peas (or asparagus tips) and cook until *al dente*.
5. Toss the sauce with the pasta, sprinkle with grated cheese, and serve.

Gramigna alla Salsiccia

Pasta with Sausage

Serves 8

Gramigna is a traditional Bolognese pasta, shaped like a short, thin, curly spaghetti with a hole in the center. It can be made by pressing dough through an extruder pasta maker with a gramigna die, or just like in the old days when it was shaped with a long needle. In Bologna, gramigna is always served with sausage. They say it is a marriage made in heaven; however, you can substitute any shape of fresh pasta.

Steps and Procedures

1. In a large 12-inch sauté pan, cook the onion in the oil until the onion is transparent. Add the prepared sausage and brown over high heat for 10 minutes, breaking it up with a fork as it cooks.
2. Add the porcini mushrooms, reserving the soaking liquid. Add the salt and pepper. Cook for another 5 minutes.
3. Add the reserved strained porcini soaking liquid, Worcestershire sauce, and cognac.
4. Add the cream, slowly incorporating it with the hot sauce.
5. Season to taste. Bring the sauce to a boil and reduce liquid over high heat until the sauce coats the back of a spoon.
6. Heat water to a boil in a large 8-quart stockpot. Add salt, then the pasta. Cook until pasta is *al dente* (5 minutes). Drain the pasta and toss it with the prepared sausage sauce. Sprinkle with grated cheese and serve.

1 small onion, peeled and chopped

2 tablespoons extra-virgin olive oil

1 pound sweet Italian sausage, without casing

¼ cup dried porcini mushrooms, soaked in water

1 teaspoon sea salt

½ teaspoon freshly ground white pepper

2 tablespoons Worcestershire sauce

1 tablespoon cognac

1 cup heavy whipping cream

Salt for seasoning pasta cooking water

1 pound fresh gramigna or any other type of pasta

½ cup freshly grated Parmigiano Reggiano cheese

Carpaccio di Funghi

Marinated Portobello Mushrooms

Serves 6

4 to 5 large portobello
mushrooms
½ cup extra-virgin
olive oil
2 garlic cloves, peeled
and minced
1 tablespoon shredded
fresh basil
1 teaspoon white wine
vinegar mustard
½ cup balsamic
vinegar
1 tablespoon honey
1 teaspoon sea salt
1 teaspoon freshly
ground black
pepper
1 pound romaine
lettuce
Freshly grated
Parmigiano
Reggiano for
garnish

In Italy, this great appetizer is made with wild mushrooms such as porcini. Since it is so difficult to find those here in the United States, I have made it with portobello mushrooms. I have also served it on top of grilled polenta instead of greens and sprinkled Gorgonzola cheese crumbles over it.

Steps and Procedures

1. Remove the stems from the portobellos, gently wash the caps, and remove the black gills with a spoon.
2. Fire up the grill and brush the tops of the mushrooms with olive oil. Grill mushroom caps for 5 minutes on each side. Remove and slice them thin.
3. Prepare the vinaigrette dressing by placing the garlic and basil in a food processor to mince. Add the mustard, vinegar, honey, salt, and pepper. Slowly add the oil while the machine is running.
4. Wash, spin, and trim the romaine and tear it into pieces. Place them on a large platter, and top with the grilled mushrooms. Sprinkle the dressing on top and sprinkle top with grated cheese. Chill until ready to serve.

Faraona al Forno

Oven-Roasted Guinea Hens

Serves 8

Guinea hens have a milder flavor than other game birds because they are farm-raised. My father was an avid hunter in the old days and used to bring home many game birds and my Nonna would cook them for the whole family.

Steps and Procedures

1. Clean the birds inside and out. Rinse them and pat them dry. Put ½ onion, ½ orange, butter, sage, and rosemary, salt, and pepper in the cavity of each bird. Sprinkle salt all over the birds; then place the slices of pancetta on top of the birds.

2. Preheat the oven to 400°F.

2. Truss the birds and lay them in a roasting pan. Sprinkle with brandy and stock. Cover the pan with foil, then roast in the oven for 50 minutes, or until 170°F. is reached on an instant-read thermometer.

3. About 10 minutes before the birds are ready, remove the bacon from the breasts and baste the birds with pan juices.

The Hens

2 guinea hens, about 2 pounds each

1 onion, peeled and cut in half

1 orange, cut in half

4 tablespoons unsalted butter

8 fresh sage leaves

2 sprigs fresh rosemary

1 teaspoon sea salt plus extra for seasoning outside of birds

1 teaspoon freshly ground black pepper

6 thin slices pancetta

1 cup chicken stock

¼ cup brandy

See page 76 for Sauce Ingredients

The Sauce

*2 tablespoons
   unsalted butter*
*1 leek, washed and
   trimmed, sliced
   very thin*
*3 garlic cloves, peeled
   and minced*
*1 teaspoon fresh
   minced Italian
   parsley*
*¼ cup finely chopped
   prosciutto*
¼ cup brandy
*1 cup fresh orange
   juice*

4. In a small 2-quart saucepan, put the butter, leek, garlic, parsley, and prosciutto. Cook for 5 minutes over high heat. Add the brandy and orange juice and cook the sauce over medium heat for 15 minutes.

5. When the birds are ready, remove them from the pan, cut each into 8 pieces, and set them aside. Strain the pan drippings and add them to the sauce. Bring the sauce to a boil and reduce it by half. Taste and adjust seasoning. Spoon the sauce over the birds and serve at once.

Spezzatino con Piselli e Patate

Veal Stew with Potatoes and Peas

Serves 8

Buy a whole veal roast from a reputable butcher, and cut it yourself into 2-inch cubes. The extra effort will pay off in the end, because you will be able to control the quality of your meat. I use a combination of olive oil and butter when cooking meat to achieve a better flavor.

Steps and Procedures

1. In a large 6-quart sauté pan, melt 2 tablespoon of the butter and the olive oil. Season the veal with salt and pepper. Add the prepared veal to the pan in small batches, and brown well on all sides. Transfer the cooked veal to a plate and repeat the process until all the meat is cooked, adding more butter and oil as needed.
2. Heat 2 additional tablespoons of butter in the casserole, add the onions and garlic and cook over low heat, stirring occasionally, until translucent.
3. Stir in the herbs: parsley, thyme, and bay leaves. Add the cooked veal plus any accumulated juices. Add the potatoes. Season with more salt and pepper. Add the stock and bring it to a boil. Reduce the heat to low, add the peas, and simmer until the veal is tender about ½ hour.
4. Transfer the meat to a dish and keep it warm. Reduce the liquid to 2 cups. Strain and reserve.
5. In a small saucepan, bring the milk to a boil. In a medium nonreactive saucepan, melt the remaining 3 tablespoons of butter. Add the flour and whisk over high heat. Gradually whisk in the milk and bring it to a boil, whisking constantly until it thickens. Add the cooking liquid.

5 tablespoons
   unsalted butter
2 tablespoons
   extra-virgin
   olive oil
3 pounds boneless veal
   shoulder, trimmed
   and cut into
   2-inch cubes
1 teaspoon sea salt
1 teaspoon freshly
   ground white
   pepper
2 medium onions,
   peeled, and finely
   chopped
3 garlic cloves, peeled
   and finely minced
¼ cup chopped fresh
   Italian parsley
½ teaspoon fresh
   thyme sprigs
2 bay leaves
4 potatoes scrubbed,
   peeled, and cubed

(Continued)

*3 cups (beef or veal)
stock
1 cup frozen peas
1 cup milk
3 tablespoons all-
purpose flour
⅛ teaspoon grated
nutmeg
¼ cup fresh lemon
juice
1 teaspoon minced
fresh rosemary*

6. Simmer over low heat until the sauce thickens (about 15 minutes). Stir in the lemon juice and season with the nutmeg and additional salt and pepper.
7. Spoon the sauce over the veal, sprinkle with rosemary, and serve.

Castagnaccio di Uvetta e Pinoli

Chestnut Flat Bread with Raisins and Pine Nuts

Serves 6

Chestnut trees line the hillsides of Bologna and during fall a variety of dishes made with chestnuts are popular. My grandmother used to make this dish for our snack. Italian import stores usually carry chestnut flour.

Steps and Procedures

1. In a large bowl, incorporate the flour with the water, salt, baking soda, and oil. Stir in the raisins and pine nuts. Make a thick batter.
2. Heat a 10-inch nonstick frying pan. Brush with vegetable oil and heat. When the oil is hot, drop a spoonful of batter into the pan as you would with pancake batter.
3. Cook on both sides until golden in color. Remove and serve.

1¼ cups chestnut flour
1 to 2 tablespoons water
1 teaspoon salt
½ teaspoon baking soda
2 tablespoons olive oil
1 teaspoon golden raisins
1 tablespoon pine nuts
Vegetable oil

Chapter Three

La Cucina della Nonna Maria

Picnics at San Luca

Polpettone alla Bolognese (*Cheese Meat Loaf*)
Insalata Capricciosa (*Vegetable Salad*)
Insalata di Riso (*Cold Rice Salad Stuffed in Tomatoes*)
Erbazzone (*Savory Cheese Pie*)
Torta di Mele della Nonna (*Apple Cake*)

Making Biscotti for the Holidays

This chapter is in memory of my mother's mother.

I remember how December settled its icy fingers around my grandmother's pale yellow stone cottage. The garden I often played on in the summer was dusted with the snow that chased itself across her lawn. Although winter was cold outside and the wind howled at her windows, there was always warmth in my grandmother's kitchen. I remember sitting next to her wood-burning stove to warm my feet after playing outdoors. My grandmother would stir the logs in the stove and open the round vents to let the heat from the oven thaw my frozen toes. I remember the stark image of my tall, thin grandmother with faded white hair bent over the enormous black stove. It was as if she were a beast tamer and she alone could control the fire-breathing monster. It was from the mouth of this monster that the best biscotti came. I would sit there listening to her wonderful stories while savoring a steaming cup of caffè latte, a home-made version of cappuccino, enjoying her scrumptious biscotti. She always had plenty of these wonderful Italian cookies. I was the official tester of her sweet creations.

My grandmother would begin the holiday cooking early in December. She started by chopping and measuring all her ingredients for the season. This filled the house with aromas of vanilla, anisette, and cinnamon. Then she would begin the ritual.

My grandmother always wore an oversized white apron. It was extra long and extended well below her knees. Dressed in this strange garb, she would spread the ingredients out on the long marble table in the center of the kitchen. I would move from the stove to one of the benches lining the table and curl my feet beneath me as I watched her lightning speed. She would mix, blend, knead, roll, cut, and finally bake the biscotti. She never seemed tired; to her this was a true labor of love. Soon the house would be filled with trays and trays of cookies.

With eight children and twenty-six grandchildren, my grand-mother was always afraid she would run out of biscotti. Her cookies made the holiday. We ate them with every meal, we decorated the tree with them, and we sent them to neighbors as gifts. There was always enough to go around.

When my grandmother passed away she left each of her grandchildren something small from her house, some token of a memory she related to them. To me, she gave her biscotti recipes. Those times together in December were as special to her as they were to me.

Biscotti al Latte

Milk Cookies

Makes 24 cookies

A few tips for cookie making: Measure the ingredients accurately, use the best ingredients, always preheat the oven, only bake in the middle rack of the oven, refrigerate butter dough before shaping, use heavy cookie sheets, line cookie sheets with parchment paper or silk-pads; do not overwork the dough and do not overbake cookies.

Steps and Procedures

1. Cream the sugar, vanilla sugar, lemon zest, and butter together until well blended using an electric mixer. Add the egg and mix together.
2. Sift together the flour, salt, and baking powder. Combine the flour mixture with the butter mixture, adding a few tablespoons of milk as needed to form soft but not sticky dough. Do not overwork the mixture. Add more flour if needed.
3. Flatten the dough and wrap it in plastic wrap. Refrigerate the dough for 1 hour. Preheat the oven to 350°F.
4. Lightly dust your countertop and rolling pin with flour. Roll the dough out to ½ inch thickness. Using a round 2-inch-diameter cookie cutter, cut the dough into circles.
5. Place the cookies on a greased and floured or parchment-lined baking sheet. Brush the cookies with milk and sprinkle colored sugar on top. Bake for about 20 minutes on the middle rack of the oven. Give the cookie sheet a half turn after 15 minutes. Do not overbake the cookies.
6. Remove the cookies and transfer them to a wire rack to cool.

1 cup sifted confectioners' sugar
1 teaspoon vanilla sugar or extract
½ cup cold unsalted butter
1 large egg
2 cups all-purpose flour
½ teaspoon salt
½ teaspoon baking powder
2 to 4 tablespoons whole milk
1 teaspoon lemon zest
1 cup colored sugar

Biscotti Matti

Crazy Cookies

Makes 24 cookies

½ cup lightly toasted
  whole blanched
  almonds
½ cup granulated
  sugar
1 tablespoon unsalted
  butter, softened
1 cup all-purpose
  flour
½ teaspoon salt
⅛ teaspoon ground
  cinnamon
2 large egg whites
2 drops almond
  extract
¼ cup confectioners'
  sugar plus extra
  for handling, the
  dough

These cookies are called "biscotti matti" because the shape can be created on the spot. They can be stored in an airtight container in the refrigerator for up to 2 weeks or in the freezer for 3 months. I prefer to store my nuts in the freezer to keep them fresh. I use Chinese cinnamon when I bake; the flavor is much stronger.

Steps and Procedures

1. In the food processor fitted with steel blade, grind the almonds and granulated sugar together, stopping to scrape down the sides, processing until the nuts are finely ground. Do not overprocess. Add the butter to the nut mixture.

2. Sift together the flour, salt, and cinnamon into the nut mixture. Add the egg whites and the almond extract to the mixture.

3. Blend well until smooth and creamy. Remove the dough from the processor and form it into a flat round pad, seal it in plastic wrap, and refrigerate it for 1 hour. Preheat the oven to 350°F.

4. Roll the dough out into a long, thick rope and cut into 1-inch pieces. With your hands dusted with confectioners' sugar, roll each one into a small ball. Flatten each ball with the bottom of a glass or cookie press dusted with confectioners' sugar.

5. Place the cookies on a greased and floured or parchment-lined baking sheet. Bake for about 15 to 20 minutes on the middle rack of the oven.

6. Remove the cookies and transfer them to a wire rack to cool. Dust the cookies with additional confectioners' sugar.

Biscotti Speziati

Spice Cookies

Makes 60 cookies

For better flavor, place the spices in a mortar and use a pestle to mix them together and release their natural oils. Remember that spices only last 6 months to a year at the most. Buy small containers of spices. To make your own vanilla sugar, place 2 vanilla beans in 1 cup of sugar. Seal the container and store for 2 weeks.

Steps and Procedures

1. Cream together the shortening and sugar using an electric mixer. Add the eggs and spices and mix together
2. Sift the flour with the baking powder and salt. Add to prepared sugar mixture along with as much milk as needed to form a soft but not sticky dough.
3. Preheat the oven to 350°F. Cut dough into walnut-size pieces and roll each into a rope of medium thickness 2 inches long. Shape each rope into a *S*.
4. Place the cookies on a well greased and floured or parchment-lined baking sheet. Bake for 15 minutes on the middle rack of the oven. Do not overbake the cookies.
5. Remove the cookies and transfer them to a wire rack to cool.
6. Prepare the glaze by mixing together the sugar, milk, vanilla sugar and lemon extract. Brush each cookie with glaze.

Cookie Dough
1¼ cups Crisco
    shortening
1 cup sugar
4 large eggs
1 teaspoon cinnamon
1 teaspoon grated
    nutmeg
1 teaspoon grated
    ginger
1 teaspoon ground
    cloves
1 teaspoon ground
    anise
5 cups all-purpose flour
1 tablespoon baking
    powder
1 teaspoon salt
½ cup whole milk

Glaze
1 cup confectioners'
    sugar
1 to 2 tablespoons milk
2 drops lemon extract
1 teaspoon vanilla
    sugar

Biscotti alla Cioccolata

Chocolate Cookies

Makes 36 cookies

Cookie Dough

1 cup granulated
   sugar

1 teaspoon vanilla
   sugar

½ cup unsalted butter
   softened

2 large eggs

1 teaspoon almond
   extract

1 tablespoon strong
   coffee

2 cups all-purpose
   flour

½ cup cocoa

½ teaspoon salt

1 teaspoon baking
   soda

½ cup toasted
   hazelnuts,
   coarsely chopped

½ cup toasted slivered
   almonds

Biscotti means "twice baked" and in Italy the word biscotti is used to refer to all cookies. We have been making these particular biscotti at the cooking school for a long time, and they are everyone's favorite. The coffee intensifies the chocolate flavor, and the chocolate coating provides the perfect finishing touch. Freeze biscotti in a well-sealed container. For crisp biscotti, cook them longer the second time.

Steps and Procedures

1. In the bowl of an electric mixer fitted with a paddle, beat the sugar, vanilla sugar, and butter until creamy. Add the eggs, almond extract, and the coffee and cream well.

2. Sift together the flour, cocoa, salt, and baking powder. Combine the flour mixture with the butter mixture. Mix in a little more flour if dough is sticky. Stir in the toasted nuts.

    Preheat the oven to 400°F. Divide the dough into three equal pieces and with floured hands form each into a sausage shape. Flatten the tops.

3. Place the cookies on a parchment-lined cookie sheet. Lower the oven temperature to 350°F. and bake on the middle rack for 20 minutes, or until firm to the touch. Cool for 10 minutes, and then slice the biscotti diagonally with a serrated knife.

4. Lower the oven temperature to 300°F. Place the biscotti slices on a cookie sheet and bake for 5 minutes on each side.

5. Remove the biscotti and transfer them to a wire rack to cool for 30 minutes.

6. To prepare the decoration, melt the chocolates in a bowl, on top of a double boiler. Dip the biscotti first in semisweet chocolate, then place on parchment paper and let dry for 1 hour. Drizzle the white chocolate on top and let dry before serving.

Decoration

3 ounces white chocolate

6 ounces semisweet chocolate

Salame di Cioccolata
Chocolate Sausage Cookies
Makes 36 Cookies

8 ounces semisweet
  chocolate
6 tablespoon unsalted
  butter
2 large eggs
½ cup confectioners'
  sugar
4 cups pulverized
  biscotti
1 cup chopped toasted,
  blanched almonds
½ cup chopped glazed
  red cherries

This was my Nonna's special treat. Using all the ends of the biscotti or the broken ones, she would create for us children a wonderful cookie in the shape of salami with almond and cherries to make the illusion complete.

Steps and Procedures
1. Chop the chocolate into chunks and melt it in a double boiler. Remove it from the heat and add the butter. Mix together with a wooden spoon until smooth. Add the eggs and combine well.
2. In a large bowl, combine the sugar and cookie crumbs with the chocolate mixture. Stir in the almonds and cherries.
3. Butter 2 sheets of parchment paper. Divide the chocolate mixture into 2 pieces and place the chocolate mixture on the prepared papers and roll it each one into a salami about 16 inches long.
5. To serve, slice the roll into individual cookies. Wrap each of the chocolate salami in parchment paper and chill for 2 hours.

Biscotti alle Pesche

Peach Cookies

Makes 36 Cookies

These cookies are usually made for holidays, weddings, and special occasions. Everyone loves them. They are well worth the time and labor involved in preparing them. Shaped like peaches, made with 2 cookies joined together with chocolate ganache, then dipped in sweet liqueur and rolled in sugar. Make sure that you have an even number of cookies.

Steps and Procedures

1. Cream the sugar, vanilla, and butter together. Blend the eggs and lemon zest into the mixture.
2. Sift the flour with the salt and baking powder. Combine the flour mixture with the butter mixture. Refrigerate the dough for ½ hour.
3. Preheat the oven to 350°F. Roll the dough into small 1-inch-size balls, taking care to have an even number. Place the dough balls on a parchment-lined baking sheet. Bake for about 10 to 15 minutes.
4. Remove the cookies and let them cool on a wire rack.
5. To make the garnishes melt the chocolate in a double boiler. Stir in the heavy cream and the nuts. With a spoon, hollow out the center of the prepared cookies. Stir the cookie crumbs into the prepared chocolate ganache.
6. Fill one cookie with chocolate mixture and then join with a second one. Repeat until all the cookies are assembled. Soak the prepared cookies in the liqueur, then roll them in granulated sugar. Place them in paper cups. Add a paper leaf on the top of each or pipe on green frosting before serving.

Cookie Dough

1 cup granulated sugar
1 teaspoon vanilla sugar
½ cup unsalted butter at room temperature
3 large eggs
1 teaspoon grated lemon zest
3¼ cups all-purpose flour
½ teaspoon salt
1 teaspoon baking powder

Garnishes

8 ounces sweet chocolate
½ cup heavy cream
¼ cup toasted chopped almonds
1 cup Sloe Gin or sweet almond liqueur (amaretto)
1 cup granulated sugar
36 paper leaves

Food for Healing

Nursing is a field that combines medical science with a genuine desire to nurture and make people feel better. The same is true for the culinary art. Even though it doesn't use medical knowledge, it has the power to make people feel better. My grandmother's life's work was based on this basic concept. As a nurse and a mother of eight children, she always knew how to make you feel better, not with medicine but with her cooking and lots of nurturing. My Nonna had an innate gift. No matter what was troubling you on a particular day, after eating one of her delightful dishes, things took on a different perspective. She had a way of making us feel better. She often described her remedies as food for healing.

As a little girl, I was given sips of balsamic vinegar whenever I complained of a tummy ache. The magical potion made my ailments disappear. My Nonna's amazing power transformed my image of her into one of a fairy tale wizard. She was a chemist who knew not only how certain ingredients could alter the taste of food, but also how they could alter the way you feel. For instance, if you couldn't sleep, chamomile tea was brewed; for congestion, she would make a blend of herbs and mix it with hot milk. Garlic was used raw in salad dressings for a healthy heart and fit body. She called nutmeg the spice of life. She believed of course, in feeding a cold, so one of her delicious soups would magically appear whenever we came down with one. This remedy goes a long way toward fixing scratchy throats and stuffy noses. A combination of carbohydrates, chicken stock, and dark green leafy Swiss chard, it is truly packed full of things that are as good tasting as they are good for you. She also believed in the curative powers of dandelions, viewed by most Americans as pesky weeds. These plants have deep roots in Italian cuisine. They are used in salads, teas, and wines because they are rich in minerals and iron. What spinach is to Popeye, dandelions are to Italians.

It is not surprising to me that nowadays what is termed "healthy" or "good for you" is what my Nonna was making for me so many years ago. She used nothing raised with growth hormones or antibiotics, no irradiated foods, no products containing preservatives, and no artificial flavors like aspartame or saccharin. Only the freshest foods would do—lots of grains, legumes, vegetables, and fresh fruits. She used to tell me, moderation is the key, and not only in what you eat, but also in the way you live.

She was a chemist who knew not only how certain ingredients could alter the taste of food, but also how they could alter the way you feel.

Crescentine

Fried Dough

Serves 8

2 teaspoons active dry
yeast

2 tablespoons warm
water (95° to
110°F.)

2 cups all-purpose
flour

1 teaspoon fine sea
salt

2 tablespoons
shortening

½ cup warm whole
milk

2 cups canola oil for
frying

Crescentine were usually made during the winter months when the kitchen was warm and bread dough was left over. My grandmother was the best crescentine maker in the family, though Zia Franca ran a close second. The whole family would join in this friendly competition and volunteer as taste testers. Serve as an appetizer with cold meats and pickled vegetables, or as a snack with soft cheeses such as stracchino. The name comes from crescere, *meaning "to grow."*

Steps and Procedures

1. In a small bowl, stir the yeast into the warm water and let stand until foamy (about 5 minutes). In a large bowl whisk together flour and salt and make a well in the center.
2. Add the shortening to the well with the yeast mixture and milk. Stir it all together until it just forms a dough.
3. On a lightly floured surface with floured hands, knead the dough until smooth and elastic (about 20 minutes). Transfer the dough to a lightly oiled bowl, turning it to coat, cover with plastic wrap, and place in a warm spot away from drafts. Let the dough rise for 1 hour, or until it doubles in bulk.
4. On a lightly floured surface with a floured rolling pin, roll out the dough into a ½-inch-thick rectangle (about 10 by 8 inches).
5. With a plain pastry cutter, cut dough into two-inch diamonds or squares, transferring the dough balls, to a parchment lined cookie sheet. With a fork, mark the crescentine several times, let them rise for another 15 minutes.

6. In a large 3-quart saucepan, heat the oil over moderate heat. Working in batches, fry the crescentine, turning them occasionally, until puffed and golden brown (about 2 to 3 minutes). With a slotted spoon transfer them to paper towels to drain.

Passatelli

Bread Dumpling Soup

Serves 8

8 cups defatted beef
  stock
Salt and pepper for
  seasoning stock
2 cups fresh bread
  crumbs
½ cup all-purpose
  flour
1 cup freshly grated
  Parmigiano
  Reggiano cheese,
  plus extra for
  garnish
3 large eggs
½ teaspoon grated
  nutmeg
1 teaspoon salt
½ teaspoon freshly
  ground black
  pepper

This soup is the ultimate comfort food. Light and delicate, it has become a favorite of my family, especially during flu season. My children refer to it as the "worm" soup because of the shape of the dumplings. Use a good full-body stock and prepare the dough ahead, then shape into dumplings right before serving. I add a little flour to the dough to prevent the dumplings from breaking in the broth. Make sure that the broth is hot but not boiling when adding the dumplings. Add lemon zest to the dough for extra flavor.

Steps and Procedures

1. Heat the stock in a 6-quart stockpot (do not boil). Taste for seasoning and add salt and pepper as needed.
2. To prepare the dough, in a bowl, combine the bread crumbs, flour, cheese, eggs, nutmeg, salt, and pepper. The mixture should be firm but not dry. Add more bread crumbs if too wet—or a little broth if too dry.
3. Put the prepared dough through a ricer with large openings, or use a passatelli maker, or a food mill to form the dumplings.
4. Drop the passatelli into the hot broth and gently stir. Add cheese and adjust the seasoning, simmer over low heat for 5 minutes and then serve.

Stracciatella

Egg Drop Soup

Serves 6

This quick and easy soup was usually served in our family during the Easter season. Start with fine-quality basic ingredients: a good broth, fresh Parmigiano Reggiano cheese, and the fresh eggs available. Follow these simple techniques: heat the broth, pour the egg mixture in a little at a time, then wait a minute or two before whisking the mixture. I sometime serve this soup with asparagus tips or peas.

Steps and Procedures

1. Bring the stock to a rapid boil in a 6-quart stockpot.
2. In a large bowl, whisk together the eggs, nutmeg, and cheese.
3. A little bit at a time, add the egg mixture to the boiling stock. Cook for 2 to 3 minutes, then stir the mixture. Add the spinach, added above salt, and pepper. Simmer for 20 minutes.
4. Serve the soup with freshly grated cheese.

4 cups defatted clear chicken stock
8 large eggs
1/8 teaspoon grated nutmeg
1/4 cup freshly grated Parmigiano Reggiano cheese, plus extra for garnish
2 cups shredded spinach or Swiss chard
1 teaspoon sea salt
1/2 teaspoon freshly ground white pepper

Pollo Arrosto

Roast Chicken

Serves 8

2 whole roasting
   chickens
Sea salt to taste
Freshly ground black
   pepper to taste
2 sprigs fresh thyme
2 sprigs fresh
   rosemary
8 fresh sage leaves
4 cloves garlic, peeled
1 small onion, peeled
   and cut in half
2 lemons
¼ cup extra-virgin
   olive oil
1 cup dry white wine
1 cup chicken stock
¼ cup chopped black
   olives
4 large Russett
   potatoes peeled and
   slice lengthwise
¼ cup unsalted butter

When I was growing up, my Nonna would only cook chicken on special occasions or for our Sunday meal. I remember her outside in the yard plucking the chicken feathers off, then bringing the bird inside and using the top of the open fire to singe off the under feathers. She never used the oven to roast the chicken. Instead, she always made it right on top of the stove, using a heavy terra-cotta pot that would seal in all the juices. The aroma would travel throughout the house.

Steps and Procedures
1. Wash the hens and put them dry. Clean and season the cavities with salt and pepper and fill with the fresh herbs, garlic, and onion. Zest the lemons and squeeze the juice, then add both. Truss the chickens with their wings tips tucked under.
2. Preheat the oven to 500°F. Cut the tail off of each bird and rub the entire skin with salt and oil. Place the chickens on a V-shaped rack in a roasting pan. Roast, turning the chickens frequently, until the skin is crisp and well-browned (about 15 minutes).
3. Lower the heat to 350°F. and place the chickens on a baking dish. Drizzle with wine and stock. Add the olives and potatoes. Season with salt. Bake, basting frequently, for another 50 minutes, or until the internal temperature reaches 170°F. on an instant-read thermometer. Baste frequently.
4. Transfer the strained pan drippings to a heavy-bottomed saucepan. Cook over medium-high heat, carefully whisking in the butter. Bring the mixture to a boil. Simmer for 5

minutes. Reduce the sauce enough so that it coats a spoon lightly. Adjust the seasoning and keep the sauce warm.

5. Transfer the chickens to a work surface. Run a sharp knife under the wishbone at the front of the breast, then carefully slip the knife between each breast half and carcass. Cut boneless breast half together with the leg and thigh attached, then cut the leg off. Repeat with remaining chicken.

6. Place the chickens on a serving platter, decorate with the olives then spoon sauce over and serve.

Torta di Riso

Rice Cake

Serves 8

5 cups milk
1 cup granulated
   sugar
1 teaspoon salt
1 teaspoon grated
   lemon zest
1 teaspoon grated
   orange zest
2 cups Arborio rice
½ cup golden raisins
1 tablespoon rum plus
   additional for
   coating cake
5 large eggs
1 teaspoon vanilla
   extract
2 cups heavy
   whipping cream
1 cup toasted chopped
   almonds
1 cup crushed
   amaretti cookies

This dessert is one of my family's favorites. Easy to prepare, it can be frozen and served at room temperature. My mother even made it in her bakery in Bologna, but my Nonna Maria's version was my favorite. She always made her risotto cake on Fridays and had it ready for the weekend. This is her recipe, modified a bit to make it easier to prepare.

Steps and Procedures

1. Heat the milk in a 3-quart saucepan. Add the sugar, salt, and the lemon and orange zest. Add the rice and cook over very low heat until the milk is absorbed (about 40 minutes). Remove the pan from the heat and cool for 15 minutes. Soak the raisins in rum and reserve.

2. Preheat the oven to 350°F. Beat the eggs with the vanilla until well blended then add it to the rice mixture and mix thoroughly. Stir in the cream, almonds, and amaretti crumbs.

3. Butter and line a 9-by-13-inch baking dish with parchment paper and pour the rice mixture into it. Smooth the top, cover with foil, and bake for 1 hour or more, or until the mixture is thickened and the rice is soft.

4. Remove the cake from the oven and let it cool for 1 hour. Before serving, brush with rum.

Crostata di Mostarda

Wild Cherry Tart

Serves 8

Mostarda is a tart jelly that is regularly used in Bologna as a filling for tarts or sweet ravioli. You can use your favorite jelly and fruit combinations: apricot, peach, or plum. It can be made ahead and placed in the freezer for up to 2 weeks.

Steps and Procedures

1. Combine the flour, sugar, vanilla extract, and salt on your work surface. Using your fingertips, combine the butter with the flour mixture until it resembles coarse cornmeal. Preheat the oven to 350°F.
2. Combine the egg yolk with lemon juice, zest, and water, making a well in the flour mixture. Gently work additions in. If the dough feels dry, add a little water. Do not knead the dough or gluten will develop and the dough will become tough. Using the heel of your hand, push a section of the dough down and away against the work surface, smearing the dough to combine.
3. Gather dough into a ball and shape it into a flat, round disk. Wrap it in plastic wrap and put it in the refrigerator. Chill for 30 minutes.
4. On a well-floured board, roll out two-thirds of the dough into an 11-inch circle and, with the help of the rolling pin, transfer the dough to a 9-inch tart pan with a removable bottom. Press the dough down to fit the pan, trim any excess dough and add trimmings to the remaining dough.
5. Gently prick the pastry all over with a fork, taking care not to pierce pastry all the way through. Spread the pastry shell with jam and top with pitted cherries.

2 cups all-purpose flour
6 tablespoons confectioners' sugar plus extra for garnishing tart
¾ teaspoon vanilla extract
½ teaspoon salt
½ cup unsalted butter
1 egg yolk
1 tablespoon lemon juice
1 teaspoon lemon zest
2 to 3 tablespoons ice water
1 cup jam (cherry)
2 cups pitted sour cherries
Egg glaze, made by mixing 1 egg yolk with 1-tablespoon water

6. Roll out the remaining dough and cut it into long strips a ½-inch wide. Create a lattice design over the top of the tart. Use one long strip to line the edge of the tart. Brush with egg glaze. Bake the tart for 30 minutes. Sprinkle with confectioners' sugar and serve.

Frittelle di Mele

Apple Fritters

Serves 8

The apple fritters that my grandmother made were quite a treat. Her version is not the traditional one, but the end result is a light golden package bursting with flavor. I use a variety of firm apples: Granny Smith, Golden Delicious, Fuji, or Saga. For frying always use fresh oil and make sure it is hot before adding the fritters, no more than 5 or 6 at a time.

Steps and Procedures:

1. Sift the flour, baking powder, and salt into a medium-size bowl. In a blender or food processor, combine the eggs, milk, sugar, vanilla, and lemon juice and zest until smooth. Slowly whisk the liquid mixture into the flour mixture and stir until the batter is smooth. Cover and refrigerate for 2 hours.
2. Add the prepared apples, raisins, and walnuts to the refrigerated batter.
3. When ready to cook the fritters, heat oil in a deep 6-quart stockpot and fry several spoonfuls of the apple mixture at a time until golden brown on both sides (approximately 5 minutes). Do not let the oil get too hot or the fritters will not cook in the middle. Blot the fritters on paper towels.
4. Serve immediately sprinkled with cinnamon sugar.

1 cup all-purpose flour
1 teaspoon baking powder
1/2 teaspoon salt
2 large eggs
1/2 cup whole milk
2 tablespoons granulated sugar
1 teaspoon vanilla extract
1 tablespoon lemon juice
1 teaspoon lemon zest
6 apples peeled, cored and coarsely chopped
1/2 cup golden raisins
1/4 cup finely chopped toasted walnuts
2 cups canola or vegetable oil for frying
1 cup granulated sugar mixed with 1 teaspoon cinnamon for garnish

Pere Cotte allo Zabaglione

Pears with Custard Sauce

Serves 8

Poached Pears
3 cups dry red wine
3 cups water
1 cup sugar
1 cinnamon stick
2 whole cloves
8 firm Bosc pears
¼ cup Sweet William Pear or Grand Marnier
Fresh mint for garnish

Zabaglione Sauce
9 large egg yolks
1 cup dry Marsala wine or champagne
1 cup granulated sugar

Poached pears are the perfect ending to a sophisticated dinner party. This recipe makes a very elegant presentation. Serve the pears whole or slice them in half and fan them. Using Sweet William Pear liqueur can enhance the sauce.

Steps and Procedures

1. Put the wine, water, and sugar in a large 6-quart stockpot. Bring the poaching liquid to a boil. Boil for 5 minutes until the sugar melts. Lower the heat to a simmer and add the cinnamon stick and cloves.
2. Peel the pears, leaving them whole and taking care to leave the stem intact, then core them from the bottom using an apple corer.
3. Put the prepared pears into the poaching liquid. The pears should be covered with liquid. Add more water if necessary.
4. Poach the pears for 20 to 30 minutes, or until the flesh feels soft to the touch.
5. Remove the pears from the poaching liquid, cool, and put in the refrigerator to chill.
6. Bring the poaching liquid to a boil and cook until reduced to a cup or a coating consistency. Add the Sweet William Pear liqueur.
7. To make the zabaglione sauce, mix the egg yolks, wine, and sugar in a bowl.
8. Heat a pot of water over low heat. Place the bowl with the egg mixture over the pot of water. Cook until the mixture

is heated, test with your finger. Do not overheat or bring it to a boil. Remove the bowl from the heat and poor the mixture into the bowl of an electric mixer fitted with wire whisk.

9. Beat the mixture for 10 minutes at high speed, or until it is doubled in volume and a pale yellow color and smooth consistency.

10. To serve, coat the bottom of 8 plates with reduced sauce from the poaching liquid. Place the chilled pears on top. Drizzle with zabaglione sauce and garnish with fresh mint.

Market Shopping

*I*talian supermarkets sell everything. My sister and I would dare each other to look in the frozen meat section. Once the shock of chicken heads, pig feet, and various organs of cows had begun to subside, we'd dare each other to touch the meat. With only a thin sheet of plastic separating you from the witch-like ingredients stacked with parsley before you, this was a daunting task.

My Nonna didn't shop in the new air-conditioned supermarkets sprouting up all over Italy. She preferred to discuss her choices for dinner with the people who grew the produce or raised the meat. My Nonna always preferred the market. I liked to imagine food had been purchased this way since the time of Romans, only instead of lire the shoppers would barter with baskets of eggs or chickens.

All the vendors knew my Nonna Maria. Many of the vendors we'd encounter at the market were the children of the vendors who first met Nonna Maria. They had grown up experiencing firsthand Nonna's reputation as a serious shopper. When Nonna approached no one even tried to sell her less than perfect food. She would examine each vegetable, each fruit, before placing it in her bag and discussing price. Nonna's presence commanded an unspoken respect.

Nonna Maria's first memories were of an orphanage. She remembers routinely being visited by a distinguished gentleman who would always bring her a box of surprises. She would receive packages of fruits and little cakes and clothes. There was never a note and the man wouldn't answer any of her questions about the bearer of the gifts during his visits. He would ask her a million questions about her life, what she enjoyed, and her studies, always very intent on her answers. Then he would pat her on the head and leave. She would sneak to the front of the gate and watch him speak briefly to someone inside a large black carriage before taking the seat in front and driving it. She'd stare as long as she could and yet never saw the mysterious person inside the carriage.

One spring morning as the sun poked through the leaves of the oak trees that line the gate surrounding the orphanage the black carriage pulled up. Maria dropped the doll she was playing with and ran to the gate. The distinguished man dismounted the carriage and paused when he saw her waiting on the other side of the long black iron bars. He spoke to someone inside the carriage and approached the gate. The man entered the orphanage courtyard and told her to stand straight and look in the direction of the carriage. Suddenly the door of the carriage opened Maria stood as straight as she could knowing the mysterious person who sent her all her wonderful gifts was somewhere in the darkness of the carriage. As she stared into the blackness she noticed movement and leaned forward to get a better look.

Then from the darkness a shadow leaned forward. The woman was beautiful. She was dressed in the most beautiful clothes Maria had ever seen. The woman had a young soft face that glistened with the tears streaming from the beautiful blue eyes that stared back at Maria. The woman slowly raised an elegantly gloved hand in greeting and Maria, now crying as well, mirrored the gesture. The man handed Maria a package as the woman leaned back into the darkness of the carriage and disappeared.

Maria never saw the carriage again and a few months later a large Italian family adopted her. She would tell me that as a child she would dream the carriage would pull up to the gate as it had that morning, and instead of standing there, she would run into the carriage and the beautiful woman would take her home with her. My Nonna Maria once attempted many years later to obtain records of her birth mother but all the orphanage's records had been destroyed during the wars. Maria never found out if the beautiful mysterious woman she saw that day was her mother.

Nonna Maria lived with her adopted family until the age of

> The man handed Maria a package as the woman leaned back into the darkness of the carriage and disappeared.

sixteen. When the mother of that family died, Maria's position in the family went from being a sister to that of a servant. So she applied to enter nursing school. In Italy, a woman had to be eighteen to enter the school; however, Maria was so determined she was allowed to enter at the age of sixteen, the first in Bologna to do so. While attending nursing school, Maria met and married my grandfather Umberto. They had eight children together before Umberto died after their house was hit during an air raid bombing. Nonna worked in the psychiatric hospital to support her growing children. To save money Nonna would go to the market daily and haggle with the vendors to get the best price for the greatest amount of food. Her children never went hungry.

It was this same determination Nonna would bring with her when we went market shopping. She taught me never to accept less than perfection—not only in produce, but also in life.

Pasticcio di Pasta

Baked Pasta

Serves 6

When buying pasta, look for a good-quality Italian import: La Molisana, DeCecco, and Del Verde. Cook pasta in a large pot of water. Bring water to a boil first, then add salt; remember that salted water boils one degree higher then unsalted water. Do not add oil to the water, and do not rinse cooked pasta. Most of all, remember the pasta will wait for no one. When buying eggplants choose the long, skinny ones; They have fewer seeds and therefore are less bitter.

4 eggplants
Sea salt
1 pound ripe Roma
    tomatoes
½ cup extra-virgin
    olive oil
2 garlic cloves, peeled
1 small onion, peeled
    and chopped
1 carrot, peeled and
    minced
⅛ teaspoon crushed
    red pepper flakes
1 tablespoon fresh
    basil, chiffonaded,
    plus extra for
    garnish
¼ pound prosciutto,
    chopped
½ teaspoon freshly
    ground black
    pepper
2 cups tomato sauce
1 pound penne pasta

Steps and Procedures

1. Peel the eggplants and thinly slice them lengthwise, and then put them in a colander. Sprinkle the eggplant with salt and let drain for a few hours. Peel, seed, and chop the tomatoes.

2. Rinse under cold water and dry the eggplants well. Heat the oil in a large 12-inch nonreactive skillet and add 1 of the garlic cloves to flavor the oil; when the garlic is lightly brown, remove it from the oil and discard.

3. Sauté the eggplant slices for 5 minutes on each side until soft. Remove from the skillet and reserve.

4. Add the remaining garlic clove, minced, to the skillet along with the onion, carrot, hot pepper, fresh basil, and sauté for a few minutes. Add the prosciutto and tomatoes. Season with 1 teaspoon salt and ½ teaspoon pepper and cook for 5 minutes over high heat. Add the tomato sauce and cook for 15 minutes over medium heat.

5. Bring a large pot of water to a boil, add salt, and then stir in pasta. Cover until the water comes to a boil once again. Stir and let the pasta cook until *al dente*, about 7 minutes,

*2 roasted red peppers
peeled, cored, and
sliced
¼ cup grated
Parmigiano
Reggiano cheese
¼ cup black olives,
pitted and sliced*

according to the package directions. Drain the pasta in a large colander in the sink. Toss with some of the sauce, reserving 1 cup.

6. Preheat the oven to 400°F.

7. Line a 10-inch angel food cake pan with eggplant slices. Fill with half of the prepared pasta. Top with red peppers, cheese, and olives. Cover with remaining pasta. Press mixture in to fill the mold completely. Top with the eggplant slices and cover with plastic wrap then foil. Bake in the preheated oven for 15 minutes.

8. Cool slightly and unfold onto a serving plate. Garnish with fresh basil, cheese, and reserved tomato sauce and serve.

Zuppa di Verdura

Vegetable Soup

Serves 8

One of my favorite things to do in the summer months is to wake up early and go out to the garden. Since my father came to live with us, we have quite a large garden. I love to pick the fresh vegetables. Zucchini, with their blossoms still attached, fresh peas and beans, tender Swiss chard leaves, green beans, crisp carrots, ripe tomatoes, garlic, potatoes, leeks, basil, parsley and marjoram. They seem to have grown like magic overnight, still wet from the night dew. This recipe is my Nonna's favorite soup. She used to make it with so many vegetables that there was hardly any broth left, and as a treat would always put the leftover crust of the Parmigiano cheese in to cook with it. If any soup remained, she would put the leftover soup through the food mill or the blender the next day and puree it.

Steps and Procedures

1. In a deep 8-quart soup pot, cook the pancetta with the olive oil over medium heat until it begins to crisp. Add the leeks hot peppers, and garlic and cook over high heat for 5 minutes until soft. Add the zucchini, carrots, potatoes, peas, green beans, cannellini beans, cabbage, and Swiss chard. Sprinkle the vegetables with salt and sauté gently until they start to wilt.
2. Cover the vegetables with the stock. Add the tomatoes and bay leaves to the pot, bring the mixture to a boil, reduce the heat to a simmer, and cook for 40 minutes, partially covered.
3. Remove the cover. Add salt, pepper, basil, and marjoram. Continue simmering for an additional minutes. The soup

¼ cup minced
   pancetta

4 tablespoons extra-
   virgin olive oil

3 leeks, heavy green
   leaves removed,
   rinsed of any sand,
   and then sliced

2 small dried hot
   peppers, crushed

2 garlic cloves, peeled
   and minced

3 zucchini, cubed

3 carrots, peeled and
   cubed

3 Idaho potatoes,
   peeled and cubed

1 cup fresh peas

2 cups fresh green
   beans, each cut
   into thirds

1 cup canned white
   canellini beans,
   rinsed

1 cup cored and thinly
   sliced cabbage

(Continued)

La Cucina della Nonna Maria

2 cups trimmed and shredded Swiss chard

1 teaspoon sea salt, plus additional to taste

3 quarts all-purpose stock

2 cups peeled, seeded, and chopped tomatoes

2 bay leaves

1 teaspoon freshly ground black pepper

1 teaspoon chopped fresh basil

½ teaspoon fresh marjoram

1 tablespoon chopped fresh Italian parsley

Freshly grated Parmigiano Reggiano cheese for garnish (about ¼ cup)

should be thickened and of a stewlike texture. Season to taste with salt and pepper.

4. Just before serving, stir in the parsley. Remove the bay leaves and pass a bowl of grated cheese at the table for diners to garnish their servings as desired.

Tagliolini alle Verdure

Pasta with Garden Sauce

Serves 6

A peasant dish fit for a king. A light dish, tagliolini are flat pasta three times the width of an angel hair pasta. If the potatoes and pasta liaison leaves you wondering, you will become a believer once you taste it. The combination of flavors works well together.

Steps and Procedures

1. Bring an 8-quart pot of water to a boil. Add salt, then pasta, and cook until *al dente*, (about 7 minutes) Drain and drizzle with 1 tablespoon of the oil.
2. Heat the remaining oil in a 12-inch size skillet. Add the onion and garlic and sauté over high heat for 5 minutes. Add the carrots, celery, zucchini, peppers, potatoes, prosciutto, and tomatoes. Sprinkle the vegetables with salt. Cook over medium heat for 5 minutes.
3. Sprinkle with salt and pepper. Add the broth. Cook over high heat to reduce, about 10 minutes. Add the basil. Toss the pasta with the sauce. Sprinkle with cheese and serve.

Sea salt to taste as needed
1 pound fresh tagliolini or linguine
4 tablespoons extra-virgin olive oil
1 yellow onion, peeled and chopped
2 cloves garlic, peeled and minced
1 carrot, peeled and julienned
1 celery stalk julienned
2 zucchini julienned
2 sweet red peppers, julienned (sliced into thin matchsticks)
2 all-purpose potatoes, peeled and julienned
¼ pound prosciutto, julienned
6 ripe Roma tomatoes, seeded and julienned
1 teaspoon freshly ground black pepper
½ cup vegetable broth
1 teaspoon fresh basil, chiffonaded
¼ cup freshly shredded Parmigiano Reggiano cheese

Portafogli alla Bolognese

Stuffed Beef Packets with
Cornbread Stuffing in Artichoke Sauce

Serves 8

2½ pounds top round
  steak, cut into ¼-
  inch-thick slices
1 teaspoon sea salt,
  plus 1 teaspoon for
  sauce to taste
1 teaspoon coarsely
  ground black
  pepper, plus ½
  teaspoon for sauce
  to taste
¼ pound mortadella,
  sliced very thin
2 tablespoons extra-
  virgin olive oil
2 tablespoons
  unsalted butter
1 onion, peeled and
  minced
1 celery stalk, minced
2 cloves garlic, peeled
  and minced
1 cup cornbread, cut
  into small cubes
1 cup whole milk
2 large eggs

*In the spring some markets sell tender baby artichokes, use them or
frozen artichokes rather than the canned. Marinate the meats in the
wine overnight to tenderize. Use dense cornbread or semolina bread for
the stuffing.*

Steps and Procedures

1. Lay each of the beef slices on a cutting board and pound
    with a meat mallet to flatten to a uniform thickness. Be
    careful not to tear the flesh. Pat the meat dry with paper
    towels, then rub it all over with salt and pepper.

2. Put a slice of mortadella on each of the meat slices. In a 3-
    quart saucepan, heat the oil and melt the butter, add the
    onion, celery, and garlic and sauté over high heat for 5 min-
    utes. Remove the pan from the heat, add the cornbread and
    stir in the *milk*.

3. Put the cornbread in a large bowl and mix it together with
    the eggs, cheese, parsley, salt, and pepper. Reserve the pan
    for browning the meat.

4. Spoon the cornbread stuffing in a row lengthwise down
    the center of each meat slice. Starting at the long end, roll
    up each jelly-roll fashion. Tie the rolls with string every
    inch or so.

5. In the same 3-quart reserved pan set over medium-high
    heat, add the meat rolls and brown on all sides. Deglaze the
    pan with the wine and broth and cook for 15 minutes. Add
    the artichokes, olives, salt, pepper, and tomatoes, then
    lower the heat to a simmer, cover, and cook for 1½ hours, or

until the meat is tender and it reaches 145°F. on instant-read thermometer.

6. Place the meat rolls on a cutting board and let rest to cool. Remove the strings. Cut the rolls into ½-inch slices, place on a serving platter, and spoon the artichoke sauce over the top. Serve immediately.

½ cup freshly grated Parmigiano Reggiano cheese
1 tablespoon minced fresh Italian parsley
½ cup dry red wine
1 cup beef broth
1 cup defrosted artichoke hearts, sliced
¼ cup black olives, pitted and sliced

Involtini di Maria

Stuffed Veal Scaloppine

Serves 8

3 pounds veal
   scaloppine, thinly
   sliced from the top
   round of the leg
1 teaspoon sea salt,
   plus additional for
   seasoning stuffing
   and final dish
½ teaspoon freshly
   grated black
   pepper, plus
   additional for
   seasoning stuffing
   and final dish
2 cups fresh bread
   crumbs
½ cup whole milk
2 large eggs
1 cup grated
   Parmigiano
   Reggiano cheese
1 teaspoon fresh
   thyme leaves
1 tablespoon chopped
   fresh Italian
   parsley

My grandmother, Nonna Maria, always made these tender little morsels and served them with mashed potatoes. I remember going to the market with her early in the morning. As she gave instructions to the butcher on how to cut the meat, I would look in disbelief at the whole carcass hanging in the store dripping blood on the sawdust-covered floor. I swore to myself then that I would never eat meat again, only to change my mind as soon as I sat at the table and the delicious aroma of Nonna's involtini filled my nostrils.

Steps and Procedures

1. Lightly pound the scaloppine with a flat mallet; cover with plastic wrap to prevent the meat from tearing. Season each veal slice with salt and pepper and top with mortadella.
2. In a small bowl, mix together the bread crumbs, milk, eggs, cheese, thyme, parsley, nutmeg, salt, and pepper. Keep the mixture moist with ¼ cup of the prepared stock.

3. Place a spoonful of bread mixture on top of each veal slice. Roll each up and secure with a toothpick, or tie with string.

4. Melt the butter and oil in a 12-inch sauté pan and cook the onion, celery, and drained porcini (reserve the liquid) until the onion is transparent.

5. In the sauté pan brown the veal involtini on all sides. Add the wine, porcini liquid, tomato sauce, and stock and bring to a boil. Lower the heat and simmer for 45 minutes. Remove the pan from the heat and transfer the veal to a serving dish. Adjust the seasoning of the sauce with salt and pepper and serve.

⅛ teaspoon freshly grated nutmeg
2 tablespoon unsalted butter
2 tablespoons extra-virgin olive oil
1 small onion, peeled and finely chopped
1 celery stalk, finely chopped
1 tablespoon dried porcini mushrooms, soaked in water
1 cup dry white wine
1 cup tomato sauce

Pinza

Jelly Tart

Makes 2 tarts

Dough

3 large eggs
1 cup granulated sugar
8 tablespoons unsalted butter, melted and cooled
1 tablespoon olive oil
1 teaspoon lemon zest
1 teaspoon vanilla sugar or extract
4 cups all-purpose flour
1 tablespoon baking powder
⅛ teaspoon salt
1 tablespoon whole milk

Fillings

1 cup plum jelly
¼ cup golden raisins, soaked in rum, then drained
¼ cup toasted pine nuts
Egg wash made by combing 1 egg yolk with 1 tablespoon water
½ cup granulated sugar

As children one of our favorite pastimes was to collect pinecones and sit on the stoop of Nonna's house with a small round rock and crack the shell of the pinecones to enjoy the sweet flavor of pinenuts. Today, when buying pinenuts at the store, I am always surprised at the high price. The dough can be made ahead and a variety of fillings can be used. In Bologna, for Carnival (Mardi Gras) we make pinza in individual sizes.

Steps and Procedures:
1. Preheat the oven 350°F.
2. In the bowl of an electric mixer fitted with the flat paddle, beat the eggs with the sugar until light and creamy. Add the butter and mix. Add the oil, lemon zest, and vanilla and beat until pale yellow in color. Sift the flour with the baking powder and salt; slowly add to the egg mixture. Add milk as needed. The dough should be soft but not sticky. Do not overwork it or the gluten will develop. Divide the dough into 2 pieces. Wrap each in plastic and refrigerate for 1 hour.
3. Lightly flour a cutting board and rolling pin. Roll out each piece of dough into an oval shape about 8 inches long, 10 inches wide, and ½ inch thick.
4. Fill the center of each tart with half the jelly and top with half of the well-drained raisins and pine nuts.
5. Fold the dough into thirds, envelope style. Pinch dough and place on a cookie sheet lined with parchment paper. Brush each pinza with egg glaze and sprinkle with sugar.
6. Bake for 30 to 40 minutes, until lightly brown in color. Remove and cool before serving.

Picnics at San Luca

Rising from the highest peak in the Bolognese hills called the Colle della Guardia, "Guard Hill," sits a red basilica with a religious aura famous throughout the region. The basilica, built in the twelfth century, draws the wealthy as well as the poor, the saints as well as the sinners. At the center of this religious fervor is a painting of Mary and Child. The painting, thought to be the creation of Saint Luke, carries mystery to this day.

Legend has it that the Madonna was a gift from Oriental ambassador Teocle to the Italian senate, supposedly purchased somewhere in Constantinople. The painting has an unusually dark canvas. The Madonna and child Jesus peer out from tiny windows. The Madonna is a mysteriously dark figure. She looks out from behind her jeweled encasement with piercingly sad eyes. The rest of the painting is covered with an ornate relief of angels and decorative scrolls bathed in gold, silver, gems, and pearls.

The Madonna is carried from San Luca down 3½ kilometers of portico-covered steps to the cathedral in Bologna each year for the Feast of the Assumption. Nonna Maria, however, chose to make the pilgrimage several times a year. To entice her grandchildren to accompany her, Nonna would make the pilgrimage into an afternoon outing, a picnic.

Nonna created a game out of the adventure, not allowing us to know the contents of the picnic basket until after we had made the journey and sat through the Mass at the basilica. She would ban all from her home the day before the pilgrimage. Nonna would prepare the picnic feast and refrigerate it overnight to make sure it was well chilled. She would keep the meal simple and easy to transport but she would give each dish an elegant touch by adding fresh fruits, vegetables, and herbs or by using colorful dishes. Nonna would always put something new or different in her picnic feast.

We would take the bus to edge of Bologna near the soccer stadium. Then, we would purchase tickets and ride the red cable car up to San Luca. During Mass I would attempt to peak inside Nonna's basket to discover what treats we would be soon enjoying. While staying attentive to the service, Nonna could still protect her secret until the basilica bells herald the end of Mass. Although I was always happy to visit the beauty of San Luca, the real draw was the prospect of sitting on the lawn outside the basilica and savoring the ever-changing contents of Nonna's picnic basket.

San Luca stays frozen in time. It remains a quiet retreat from the city. Although the cable car no longer exists, the journey to San Luca is a beautiful one and still evokes in me that feeling of anticipation.

Polpettone alla Bolognese

Cheese Meat Loaf

Serves 8

Meat loaf with a twist. My students call it the Bolognese version of their favorite common dish. Serve it sliced with mashed potatoes or cold as a pâté. Use a variety of meats for to achieve a better flavor. I like to grind my own meat, but a mixture of store-ground veal, beef, and pork also leads to great results. My grandmother always saved the broth used to cook the polpettone to make a delicious soup. Because of the moist cooking method for polpettone you can use very lean meats.

1 pound veal shoulder
1 pound beef round
1 pound pork loin
1 teaspoon sea salt
½ teaspoon freshly ground black pepper
½ teaspoon freshly grated nutmeg
¼ pound mortadella
4 large eggs
2 cups fresh bread crumbs
1 cup freshly grated Parmigiano Reggiano cheese
1 teaspoon chopped fresh Italian parsley
¼ cup whole milk
1 large onion, chopped
2 celery stalks chopped
1 carrot, chopped

Steps and Procedures

1. Trim the veal, beef, and pork meat of all tendons and sinew. Cut all into 1-inch pieces. Season with salt, pepper, and nutmeg. Chill in the refrigerator for 1 hour.
2. Grind meat and mortadella twice in the meat grinder; do not use a food processor. If you do not have a meat grinder, ask the butcher to do it for you. Add the eggs, bread crumbs, cheese, parsley, and enough milk to make the mixture moist. Cook a small patty of meat and adjust for salt and pepper. With wet hands, mix the ingredients together.
3. Double a piece of cheesecloth or oil a piece of parchment paper. Take the meat mixture and shape it into a loaf. Wrap the loaf with cheesecloth or parchment paper, taking care to make a smooth, tight package. Tie with butcher's string.
4. Bring 2 quarts water to a boil. Add the meat loaf package, onion, celery, and carrot and cook at a simmer for 1¾ hours. Remove the meat loaf from the broth and cool before removing the cloth and slicing it.
5. Serve it cold with Insalata Capricciosa (recipe follows) or hot with mashed potatoes and seasonal vegetables.

Insalata Capricciosa

Vegetable Salad

Serves 8

6 potatoes in their
   jackets, well-
   scrubbed
1 pound green beans,
   trimmed
2 carrots, peeled
1 lemon
1 teaspoon white wine
   mustard
1 teaspoon chopped
   fresh Italian
   parsley
1 teaspoon sea salt
1/2 teaspoon freshly
   ground black
   pepper
1/2 cup extra-virgin
   olive oil
1 cup pancetta, cut
   into julienne
2 garlic cloves, peeled
   and minced
1/2 red onion, peeled
   and sliced thin
1 tablespoon red wine
   vinegar

A lemony potato salad without mayonnaise! My Nonna always made this salad for our picnics. She would make it the night before and let it marinate overnight. If you use bacon instead of pancetta, blanch it first in boiling water.

Steps and Procedures
1. Put the potatoes in a large pot filled with cold water, bring the water to a boil, and cook until fork-tender (about 20 minutes). Drain and cool, then peel and slice the potatoes.
2. Put the green beans and carrots in a separate pot of cold water. Bring it to a boil and cook for 8 minutes, then put it in a cold water bath to chill.
3. To prepare the dressing, remove and grate the zest and squeeze the juice of the lemon into a bowl. Stir in the mustard, parsley, salt, and pepper. Slowly, while whisking, add the oil. In a 10-inch sauce pan, cook the pancetta, garlic, and onion until soft. Sprinkle in the vinegar. Reserve.
4. Toss potatoes and vegetables with the prepared dressing, and put the bowl into the refrigerator to marinate for at least 30 minutes, or overnight.
5. Serve chilled as a side dish.

Insalata di Riso

Cold Rice Salad Stuffed in Tomatoes

Serves 8

Rice salads are a must at picnics. They are a great choice because they can be prepared a day ahead and refrigerated. For better flavor, cook the rice in advance. Use Arborio rice and wash it in a small strainer until it rinses clear. Cooking proportions: 2 parts water or stock to 1 cup rice. Cook until al dente, *about 20 to 25 minutes. For the best flavor, toss the cooked rice with dressing while it is still hot. Put the finished salad in the refrigerator to cool.*

Steps and Procedures

1. Put the onion, garlic, red and green peppers, carrots, celery, olives, prosciutto, peas, and the rice in a large bowl.
2. Cut the tomatoes in half, then core and hollow them to remove as much meat as possible without damaging the skins. Sprinkle salt on the tomatoes. Place the prepared tomatoes upside down on paper towels to drain. Next sprinkle the tomatoes with 1 tablespoon of the oil.

1 red onion, peeled and diced
2 cloves garlic, peeled and diced
2 sweet red peppers, cored and diced
2 green peppers, cored and diced
2 carrots, peeled and diced
2 stalks celery, trimmed and diced
¼ pound prosciutto, diced
1 cup pitted green olives, sliced
½ cup cooked peas
2 cups cooked rice, such as Arborio, chilled
8 vine ripe red salad tomatoes, cored and seeded
½ cup extra-virgin olive oil

(Continued)

¼ cup white wine
vinegar

1 teaspoon white wine
mustard

1 teaspoon chopped
fresh basil

1 tablespoon chopped
fresh Italian
parsley, plus whole
sprigs for garnish

1 teaspoon sea salt,
plus additional for
seasoning
tomatoes

1 teaspoon freshly
ground black
pepper

¼ cup freshly grated
Parmigiano
Reggiano cheese

3. Prepare a vinaigrette by mixing together the vinegar, mustard, basil, parsley, salt, and pepper. Slowly, while whisking, add the remaining oil.

4. Toss the rice and vegetable mixture with the prepared vinaigrette, sprinkle with cheese, then let it marinate at least 1 hour in the refrigerator.

5. Fill each prepared tomato half with a heaping serving of rice salad. Decorate the top of each with a sprig of fresh parsley. Serve as an appetizer or side dish.

Erbazzone

Savory Cheese Pie

Serves 8

This is a versatile savory pie that my grandmother would make the day after she made the fresh ricotta. She would start by bringing whole milk to a boil then adding vinegar to it, and within seconds the white cheese would rise to the top. She would then place it in a perforated ceramic mold lined with cheesecloth to drain off the liquid. Many times she would take some of the warm mixture and mix it with a little sugar and vanilla for me. What a wonderful, creamy treat. It tasted even better then pudding. Erbazzone can be made up to two days ahead and kept in the refrigerator.

The Dough

3 cups all-purpose flour

1 teaspoon sea salt

8 tablespoons extra-virgin olive oil

5 to 6 tablespoons ice water

2 whole eggs

See page 126 for Filling Ingredients

Steps and Procedures

1. Combine the flour and salt on your work surface. Add the oil to the flour and work them together until a coarse meal is formed. Next combine the flour mixture with the water and eggs. If the dough feels dry, add more water by droplets.

2. Gather the dough into a ball using the heel of your hand, then push a section of the dough down and away against the work surface, smearing the dough to combine.

3. Gather again and repeat once or twice more to achieve a smooth dough. Chill for 20 to 30 minutes before rolling it out. In the meantime, prepare the filling.

4. In a 10-inch sauté pan cook the onions slowly in the oil until they begin to soften. Add the Swiss chard and cook until soft. Season with salt and pepper. Remove from the heat and place the mixture in a bowl to cool.

5. Beat the eggs thoroughly with the ricotta, parsley, and

The Filling

*1 large yellow onion,
peeled and chopped*

*1 tablespoon extra-
virgin olive oil*

*2 cups Swiss chard,
trimmed, rolled,
and cut into strips*

*1 teaspoon sea salt,
plus additional to
taste*

*1 teaspoon freshly
ground white
pepper, plus
additional to taste*

2 large eggs

*2 cups whole milk
ricotta cheese*

*½ cup freshly grated
Parmigiano
Reggiano cheese*

*⅛ teaspoon freshly
grated nutmeg*

*1 tablespoon chopped
fresh Italian
parsley*

*Egg wash made by
combining 1 egg
yolk with 1
tablespoon water*

Parmigiano cheese. Season with salt, pepper, and nutmeg and stir into the cooled onion-chard mixture.

6. Preheat the oven to 400°F. Divide the dough into 2 pieces, 1 slightly larger then the other. Roll out 1 piece of dough to make an ⅛-inch-thick 10-inch circle. Transfer the dough to a well-buttered 9-inch cake pan. Spread the ricotta mixture on top and roll out the second piece of dough to a 9-inch circle. Cover the pie with it. Pinch the edges to seal, brush with egg wash. Lower the heat to 350°F. and bake for about 45 minutes, or until golden brown.

Torta di Mele della Nonna

Apple Cake

Serves 8

This cake is best when made with freshly picked firm, juicy apples. Nonna Maria made this cake with apples from her orchard and I loved to peek in the oven door and watch the dough rise and make the apples disappear. This is my husband's favorite dessert. It reminds him of an apple cake that his grandmother used to make. This is the perfect dessert for fall.

Steps and Procedures

1. In an electric mixer, cream together the butter and the sugar. Add the eggs and beat until they are pale yellow and ribbons form.
2. Preheat oven to 350°F. Sift the flour with the salt and baking powder.
3. Add the flour mixture and the milk to batter. Add vanilla, nutmeg, and cinnamon. With a spatula fold in the prepared apples, raisins (reserving the soaking liquid), and almonds.
4. Butter and flour 9-inch-by-13-inch baking pan. Pour the batter into the prepared pan.
5. Bake in the preheated oven for 40 to 45 minutes, or until golden brown.
6. Remove the cake and let it cool. Brush with the reserved liqueur soaking liquid. Cool and serve with your favorite ice cream.

6 tablespoons unsalted butter
1 cup granulated sugar
3 large eggs
2 cups all-purpose flour
1 teaspoon salt
1 teaspoon baking powder
½ cup whole milk
2 teaspoon vanilla sugar or extract
½ teaspoon freshly grated nutmeg
1 teaspoon ground cinnamon
5 or 6 Rome apples, peeled, cored, and sliced
½ cup golden raisins, soaked in Amaretto liqueur, then drained, reserving the liquid
¼ cup slivered toasted almonds

La Cucina della Mamma

Torta di Mandorle di Frutta
(*Almond Torte with Fresh Fruit*)

Making
Risotto

Risotto
Risotto al Pomodoro
(*Risotto with Fresh Tomato and Basil Sauce*)
Risotto alla Rucola (*Risotto with Arugola and Gorgonzola Cheese*)
Agnello al Rosmarino (*Lamb Stew with Rosemary Potatoes and Olives*)
Bollito con Salsa Verde
(*Steamed Fillet with Caper and Parsley Sauce*)
Crocchette di Semolino (*Semolina Dumplings*)
Gnocchi di Crema (*Fried Sweet Cream*)
Mistocchine (*Sweet Rolls*)

The Birthday Cake

*P*iazza Maggiore echoed with the shouts of men and the pounding of hammers as the enormous stage slowly came to life. This was to be the largest concert held in the ancient square, a celebration of both singer and city. It was in honor of Francesco Guccini, a famous Bolognese singer. He was to give a free concert in the Piazza Maggiore for his birthday—a gift to his city. As a thank-you gesture, the Bolognese Association of Bakers offered to create for him the largest birthday cake ever assembled.

As the stage grew near the city hall building, a small platform was erected next to the Fountain of Neptune in the northern corner of the square. All afternoon white trucks had been unloading sheets and sheets of cake for the celebration. It had taken ten days to bake everything. When finished the cake would be seven layers, twelve feet high, and weighing a total of a 2,500 pounds—the largest cake ever made. It took 4,880 eggs, 250 pounds of almond paste, 130 pounds of pastry decoration, 130 pounds of pastry cream, and 30 pounds of chocolate decorations, including a guitar made entirely of chocolate. My mother and I were two of only twenty chefs chosen to create this record-setting cake.

All day the work to construct this work of art continued. The sheets of cake were decorated with almond paste and surrounded by white tower decorated with chocolate music notes. Pastry arches held up each layer, and the entire cake was topped with an oversized chocolate guitar.

The pastry chefs took turns standing watch over the cake as night began to fall and the piazza began to fill. When the first notes from Guccini's guitar floated from the stage, the piazza was holding more than 150,000 people. Promoters had expected a crowd only one-fourth that size, so the chairs originally set up for the audience were lost in the sea of fans.

This chapter is dedicated to my relationship with my mother. She was once the only female master pastry chef in the Bologna Association of Bakers. Her pasticceria made her famous. She had her own television show and was often on the radio discussing her recipes. The time I spent with my mother was always food-related.

When finished
the cake would
be seven layers,
twelve feet high,
and weighing a
total of a 2,500
pounds

The steps of the church spilled over with people. The rooftops of the buildings surrounding the square were crowded with spectators. Even the fountain itself had people hanging off of Neptune trying to catch a glimpse of Guccini and his cake.

I stood close to my mother, intimidated by the swaying crowd, and tried to concentrate on the instructions the cake director was shouting over the music. When Guccini ended the concert, he was to walk to the cake platform and climb a ladder to blow out his candles and cut the first piece of cake from the top layer. We were then to take over the distribution of the cake to the crowd. The director instructed us to cut two-ounce pieces to ensure most people got cake (we were not aware at that time just how many people had come to the concert). The plan sounded well thought out and with a little more confidence I was able to relax and enjoy the concert from my privileged spot.

My easiness soon drained away, along with the color on my face as the concert came to a crashing end. Guccini finished singing and the crowd was left screaming. As he left the stage to walk the short distance to the cake platform, the crowd reacted quickly. Believing they would be able to touch Guccini, the crowd pushed forward towards him. Panic and chaos resulted. The mob trampled forward, rushing the stage. Guccini's guards whisked him backstage and away. The crowd, thinking as we were, that Guccini would eventually make it to the cake platform, shifted their direction to the cake. The chefs stood like an island in a sea of people, readying themselves for a tidal wave.

The police assigned to protect the cake jumped up on the platform to save themselves from being trampled. The platform rocked with the momentum of the people. Shouts filtered through the uproar: "Don't Push!" I heard. "Get the cake!" someone else screamed. "We want Guccini!" others chanted. I stood wide-eyed and scared. Someone shoved a piece of cake in my hand and yelled, "Start serving."

I looked around me. The chefs were trying to calm the throng by passing out pieces of cake. No longer concerned with exact measurements, the chefs were scooping cake with their hands, plopping pieces on paper plates and flinging the plates into the crowd. The police who had been unsuccessful at keeping the mob at bay, had greater success at passing out cake.

As luck would have it, the crowd calmed and slowly began to disperse. Their disappointment in not getting to touch Guccini seemed appeased by having a piece of his birthday cake. Only in Italy can you calm storming mobs with food.

La Torta Farcita

Rum Torte

Serves 12

Cake

8 large eggs at room
 temperature,
 separated
8 tablespoons
 unsalted butter, at
 room temperature
2 cups granulated
 sugar
2 tablespoons water
1 teaspoon vanilla
 extract or powder
1 teaspoon finely
 grated lemon zest
 and juice
1/8 teaspoon salt
3 1/2 cups cake flour
2 teaspoons baking
 powder

Rum Simple Syrup

1 cup water
1 cup sugar
1/2 cup dark rum

Special occasions like birthdays, graduations, or anniversaries are the perfect excuse to prepare this great cake. It can be made ahead, placed in the freezer well wrapped and then on the day of the event can be decorated and served. You can substitute orange juice for the rum. Be extra careful with the recipe for the butter cream. Make sure that the egg-white mixture is completely cool before adding the butter or it will separate. If it does separate, put it in the refrigerator for 1 hour, then add 1/2 cup vegetable shortening and beat in a mixer until creamy. My mother prepared this cake for all of my birthday parties. No wonder they were so successful!

Steps and Procedures

1. To make the cake, put your rack in the middle of the oven. Preheat the oven to 350°F. Grease and flour or line with circles of parchment paper 3 round baking pans (one 6-inches, one 8-inches and one 10-inches).

2. Separate the eggs. In a large bowl using an electric mixer, work the butter until creamy, slowly adding 1 cup of the sugar, stopping the mixer once in a while to scrape down the sides of the bowl, until the mixture is light and fluffy (about 5 minutes). Add the egg yolks one at a time, beating well after each addition, until the mixture is pale yellow and ribbons form. Add the water, vanilla, lemon juice, and zest.

3. In a large bowl, using an electric mixer, whip the egg whites and salt for 2 minutes. Slowly add the remaining cup of sugar and beat until stiff peaks form. Using a rubber spatula, gently fold one-third of the whites into the

egg-yolk mixture to lighten it. Fold in the remaining egg whites in two additions. Sift the flour and baking soda into the cake batter, then gently fold it in.

4. Divide the cake batter between the three prepared pans, smooth the surfaces, and bake for 25 minutes the 6-inch cake, 30 minutes for the 8-inch cake, and 35 minutes the 10-inch cake, or until the cake springs back when pressed.

5. Allow the cakes to cool in their pans for 15 minutes. Remove the cakes from the pans invert them on top of the pans. Remove the parchment paper and cool thoroughly before continuing the torte.

6. To make the rum syrup, in a small 2 quart saucepan, bring the water and sugar to a boil. Cook for 10 minutes, or until the sugar is dissolved. Remove the pan from the heat and stir in the rum.

7. To prepare the butter cream, in a double boiler, heat the egg whites and granulated sugar until the sugar is barely dissolved; do not overheat or the eggs will scramble. In an electric mixer, filled with a whip attachment, whip the egg whites and sugar mixture until the mixture becomes cool to the touch. While machine is running, add bits of butter and confectioners' sugar until all is incorporated.

8. To make the pastry cream, in a saucepan heat the milk with a piece of lemon zest for flavor; do not let the milk come to a boil. In a separate bowl, mix together the egg yolks, vanilla, cornstarch, and sugar. Slowly add the milk, taking care to temper it first. Add ½ cup of the milk into the egg mixture, stir, and then stir in the remaining milk. Place the pan back on top of the stove and whisk over medium heat until the mixture thickens (about 15 minutes). Remove the pan from the heat and spread on a cookie sheet covered with plastic wrap to prevent a skin from forming on the top and cool in the refrigerator until ready to use.

9. It is now time to assemble the cake with its decorations. Put the melted chocolates in a pastry bag fitted with a plain tip.

Butter Cream

8 eggs whites
1½ cups granulated sugar
7–8 cups confectioners sugar
¾ pound unsalted butter, at room temperature

Pastry Cream

4 cups whole milk
1 whole piece lemon zest
8 egg yolks
2 teaspoons vanilla sugar
6 tablespoons cornstarch
1 cup granulated sugar

Decorations

8 ounces semisweet chocolate, melted
4 ounces semisweet chocolate shaved
21 ounces Odense marzipan
¼ cup each cornstarch and powdered sugar

10. To assemble the torte, cut each cake layer in half and brush both sides with rum syrup. Cover each bottom half with cooled pastry cream topped with shaved chocolate.

11. Cover each bottom half with a top half. Put each cake on a cardboard cake base. Trim the cake tops and sides as necessary. Cover each cake with prepared butter cream, using a metal spatula. Put the cakes in the refrigerator to chill. Place extra butter cream in a pastry bag with star tip. Reserve.

12. Soften and roll out the marzipan so that it is ⅛ inch thick then sprinkle it with cornstarch and confectioners sugar. Cover each cake with marzipan, cutting off any excess, and rolling it out to use for decorations.

13. Put the smaller cake on top of the medium cake, and the medium cake on top of the large cake. Decorate the torte with the reserved butter cream on the borders and a melted chocolate design on top. Finish with marzipan decorations and extra shaved chocolate, if desired.

14. Refrigerate until ready to serve.

Early Morning Baking in the Bakery

When I was a child, I would wake to the soft sounds of my mother dressing in the next room. The world around me was cloaked in darkness and the streets outside my window were silent. The crispness of air on my nose made me debate whether to venture out from my warm cocoon of sheets and blankets or snuggle in for another dream and wait for the sun to wake me. But I would will myself to throw off the covers and hurry to get ready so I could accompany my mother as she began the day of baking. My mother believed in starting fresh each day, so she'd wake at an hour when some people were just getting to bed. She'd dress and walk to the bakery to begin mixing the batter, kneading the dough, and baking so everything would be fresh and still warm when the customers entered the store for a cappuccino and pastry on their way to work. It was wonderful to hear the rest of the world yawn itself awake. The noise of the morning would build until the sound of my father opening the store gate trumpeted the official arrival of the morning and its first offerings.

The mornings with my mother were a selfish time for me. I had my mother's attention all to myself. She listened to every word I said as she rolled and cut, while I fingered the dough scraps into a ball. My mother was a magical creature. Because of the store and her neverending baking, I would spend most of my time outside of school with my grandmother. So my time with my mother was a delicious treat. I believed my mother could do anything. She was like a magician—able to take simple things like eggs and flour and, in what seemed like no time, turn those things into incredible, delectable works of art. My mother had a gift of making for me feel a part of the morning baking. She would ask which fruit she should put on the tarts

and I'd say strawberries, then change my mind and say blue-
berries, and my mother would turn my suggestions into this
incredible rainbow of fruit on a shiny custard tart. She'd com-
pliment me on such a wonderful job. I would spend the rest of
the morning showing off my tart to the patrons and beam with
pride when any of them ordered a slice.

Although my mother originally dreamed of becoming an
opera singer, she began working in her sister's bakery and
instantly fell in love with the profession. She soon became an
apprentice at the city's most famous bakery—Pasticceria La
Canasta—and become one of the most prominent bakers in
Bologna. She was frequently featured on television shows and
in newspaper articles for her baking skills. Yet my mother was
attentive and warm whenever I needed her.

Most children idolize a superhero or a movie star, but I idol-
ized my mother. So these mornings were not only a sharing
time for us, but also a time when I could study the person. I
most wanted to emulate. Although Romans had been making
cakes as early as the second century B.C., I believed my mother
had perfected the art. She'd show me the simple techniques of
baking while revealing her secret tricks and giving me some
hints about what she had discovered through experience. I
learned to appreciate the exact science of baking and how to
accurately measure each ingredient to assure consistency.

When I return home to Bologna to visit with my family, I
like to get up early in the morning and meet my mother in her
shop as we did when I was little. We gather the ingredients and
make the morning's offerings, and for those few hours in the
early morning she still devotes all her attention to me.

Although
Romans had
been making
cakes as early
as the second
century B.C., I
believed my
mother had
perfected the
art.

Bavarese alla Fragola

Strawberry Bavarian

Serves 8

In Vicenza, Italy there is a wonderful teacher, Franca Perriz, who owns the Salsiera D'Argento Cooking School. I had the pleasure of taking several classes there. My sister, Annarita, and I took a class together. We left Bologna early one morning and drove 2½ hours to get there. We had so much fun sharing the day and learning together. This was the dessert that we made that day. The recipe here is my version, which is a combination of my mother's recipe and the one taught to us by Signora Perriz. My mother was so proud of us for showing such an interest in following in her footsteps that from that day on she prepared bavarese and sold them in the store. Customers liked the delicate light dessert, a combination of custard and heady cream that can be made in a variety of flavors. Prepared ahead, it can be frozen up to two weeks or kept in the refrigerator for a couple of days. In Italy, we use gelatin sheets instead of gelatin powder.

1 tablespoon almond or canola oil for oiling mold

¼ cup cold water

2 cup whole milk

1 vanilla bean

6 egg yolks

1 cup granulated sugar

8 ounces frozen strawberry puree

1 teaspoon vanilla extract, plus additional for the whipped cream

2 cups heavy whipping cream, well chilled

1 teaspoon confectioners' sugar

2 tablespoon unflavored gelatin

Steps and Procedures

1. Lightly oil an 8-cup ring mold. Sprinkle the gelatin over the cold water and set aside.

2. Heat the milk and vanilla bean in a small 1-quart saucepan but do not let it boil. In a 3-quart saucepan, whisk together the egg yolks and sugar.

3. Let the milk cool for a minute, then stir 1 cup of milk into the egg mixture. Once the mixture is tempered, pour in the rest of the milk while stirring.

4. Return the mixture to the stove and cook over medium heat, stirring constantly until thickened. The mixture should coat the back of a spoon when ready.

5. Remove the pan from the heat, and stir in the softened

For Decoration

*1 pint fresh
strawberries,
sliced*

*2 cups heavy
whipping cream,
whipped and put in
a pastry bag filled
with a rosette tip*

gelatin. Bring the pan back to the stove and heat for an additional minute. Do not overheat the gelatin or it will develop a grainy texture.

6. Remove the pan from the heat again and stir in the strawberry puree and vanilla extract. Cover with plastic wrap to prevent a skin from forming. Let mixture cool slightly.

7. Whip the chilled cream with the confectioners' sugar and vanilla in an electric mixer until soft peaks form.

8. Gently fold the whipped cream into the cooled egg-yolk mixture. It should be light and airy. Pour the mixture into the prepared mold.

9. Put the mold in the refrigerator to set and chill for 4 hours or overnight.

10. To unmold, dip the outside of the pan in hot water for 2 seconds, wipe the bottom dry, and invert onto a serving plate.

11. Decorate the bavarese by piping with whipped cream rosettes on the top and sides. Garnish with sliced strawberries.

Meringhe alla Panna

Meringue with Heavy Cream

Makes 12

On Sunday mornings, my mother's bakery would have lines of people waiting outside the doors to buy the fresh pastries that made the bakery famous. No matter how many meringues we would make, they were always the first to go. Prepare your meringues ahead of time; they will keep for up to a week in a sealed container at room temperature.

6 egg whites
1 cup granulated
  sugar
1 cup heavy whipping
  cream, chilled
¼ cup confectioners'
  sugar
1 teaspoon vanilla
  extract

Steps and Procedures

1. In a small bowl, combine the egg whites and the granulated sugar. Place the bowl on top of a pot of simmering water and heat to 140°F., whisking constantly. Do not overheat.

2. Remove from the heat and pour the mixture in an electric mixer bowl. Beat on high speed until the mixture is cooled and forms firm stiff peaks.

3. Place the meringue mixture into a pastry bag fitted with a large star tip. Pipe the mixture into small mounds the size of an egg on a parchment-lined baking sheet.

4. Preheat the oven to 200°F. Bake the meringues for several hours until completely dry. Remove them from the oven and cool.

5. Whip the heavy cream with the confectioners' sugar and vanilla in a chilled bowl at low speed for 3 minutes, then at high speed until stiff and firm. Make sure not to overbeat the mixture or it will turn into butter.

6. Put the whipped cream in a pastry bag fitted with a large plain tip. Pipe cream on the bottom of a cooled meringue, then top with a second meringue, and put the pastry in a paper cup. Repeat until all of the meringues are used.

Torta Ricciolina

Pasta Almond Pie

Serves 12

Dough

2 cups all-purpose
   flour
½ teaspoon salt plus
   ⅛ teaspoon
¼ cup confectioners'
   sugar
8 tablespoons
   unsalted butter,
   chilled
2 egg yolks
1 teaspoon vanilla
   extract
1 teaspoon grated
   lemon zest

This is one of my favorite Bolognese specialties. In Bologna, there are many variations of this delicious torta. This is my mother's recipe—it tastes the best, in my opinion. Make the torta a day ahead and it will have a better flavor. If using dry pasta, blanch it first in boiling, then in a cold water bath. Drain and use.

Steps and Procedures

1. Sift the flour, ½ teaspoon of the salt, and the sugar on to a work surface and make a well in the center. Add the chilled butter and work with your fingertips to form a mealy consistency.

2. Add the egg yolks, vanilla extract, and lemon zest, and gradually incorporate them with the flour, until a doughlike consistency is achieved. Add chilled water if the dough feels dry. Do not overwork the dough or it will be tough. Wrap in plastic and chill for 1 hour.

3. The first two steps can also be done in a food processor. Put flour, salt, sugar, lemon zest, and butter in the work bowl fitted with a steel blade. Process on and off until you achieve a cornmeal consistency, add the egg yolks, and process until the dough forms a ball. Gather up the ball and wrap it in plastic, and chill for 1 hour.

4. Preheat the oven to 400°F. On a floured surface roll out the dough to ⅛ inch thick. Brush the cake pan with butter, then sprinkle with bread crumbs. Line the bottom and sides of the buttered 9-by-2-inch cake pan. Fold the edges of the dough to the inside of the pan. Refrigerate for at least 30 minutes.

5. Toast the almonds in a 10-inch frying pan for 5 minutes. Transfer them to the food processor, add the sugar, and pulse until creamy.

6. On top of the dough spread half of the almond paste, lemon zest, sugar, chocolate, vanilla, and cookies.

7. Press half of angel hair pasta on top, making sure that the ingredients are well mixed. Sprinkle with liqueur and brush with butter.

8. Top with remaining almond paste, lemon zest, chocolate, vanilla, and cookies. Add one more layer of angel hair pasta, sprinkle with liqueur and brush with butter. Cover with foil and bake for 40 minutes. Remove the foil 10 minutes before the cake is done. The top should be light brown. Remove the pan from the oven and let it cool before removing the cake from the pan.

10. Dust the top of the cake with confectioners' sugar and serve.

Filling

1½ cups blanched almonds

1 cup granulated sugar

¼ cup bread crumbs and butter for preparing cake pan

1 tablespoon grated lemon zest

1 cup semisweet chocolate, finely chopped

2 tablespoons vanilla sugar

1 cup Amaretti almond cookie crumbs

8 tablespoons unsalted butter, melted

4 tablespoons Amaretto liqueur

8 ounces fresh angel hair pasta

Topping

Confectioners' sugar

Torta di Cioccolata

Chocolate Cake

Serves 8

Mousse

12 ounces semisweet
 chocolate, cut up
8 large eggs
½ cup granulated
 sugar
2 tablespoons
 Frangelico
 hazelnut liqueur
2½ cups heavy
 whipping cream,
 chilled

Cake

Melted butter and
 cocoa powder for
 preparing jelly-
 roll pan
6 large eggs
½ cup granulated
 sugar
½ cup sifted cocoa

My mother's specialty has always been cakes and tortes. The display window of her bakery was her showcase. She would change it daily and according to the holiday season. This chocolate cake is one of her favorites, and if you are a chocolate lover, you will like it, too.

Steps and Procedures

1. Melt the chocolate over a double boiler; remove the pan from the heat and reserve. Separate the eggs. Stir the yolks in the melted chocolate along with the Frangelico liqueur.
2. Mix together egg the white and sugar and heat them over a double boiler. Whip the egg whites and sugar until stiff peaks form. Whip the heavy cream into stiff peaks and refrigerate. Fold the heavy cream into the chocolate, then fold in the egg whites. Refrigerate to set.
3. Line a 10-by-14-inch jelly-roll pan with parchment paper, brush with melted butter and sprinkle with cocoa. Separate the eggs.
4. Whip the yolks with half of the sugar until the mixture is pale yellow. Whip the whites to a foam, then add the remaining sugar and whip to soft peaks.
5. Add one-third of the egg whites to the yolks, add the cocoa, then fold in the rest of whites. Spread the batter evenly on the prepared sheet.
6. Preheat the oven to 350°F. Bake the cake 20 minutes. Let it cool slightly, then sprinkle cocoa on top. Run the spatula around edges; flip over onto sheet tray lined with parchment paper.

7. To make the simple syrup, bring the water and sugar to a boil and cook for 15 minutes. Add the liqueur and cool.

8. Cut the chocolate cake into three equal pieces. Place one section on a cake board; brush with syrup; spread one-third of the chocolate mousse on top.

9. Place the second layer on top brush with syrup, and top with chocolate mousse. Cover with the third layer and brush with syrup. Cover the top and sides with chocolate mousse.

10. Press white chocolate shavings onto the sides of the cake. Top with fresh raspberries and mint leaves. Cover with plastic wrap and refrigerate for at least 2 hours before serving.

Garnish

Simple syrup made by combining 1 cup water, 1 cup sugar, and ¼ cup Frangelico liqueur

1 pint fresh raspberries

Mint leaves

White chocolate shavings

Certosino della Tilde

Christmas Chocolate Bread

Serves 8

2 cups honey
1¼ cups sugar
½ cup water
½ cup golden raisins
1 cup Marsala wine
4¼ cup all-purpose flour
2 tablespoons baking
   powder
2 tablespoons cocoa
½ teaspoon salt
1½ cups vanilla wafer
   cookie crumbs
½ cup apricot jelly
½ teaspoon ground
   cinnamon
½ teaspoon grated
   nutmeg
½ teaspoon ground
   cloves
2 teaspoons vanilla
   extract
½ cup candied orange
   peel
1 cup toasted almonds
¼ cup toasted pine nuts
8 ounces chocolate,
   coarsely chopped

My mother's name is Tilde, and this is her famous recipe for making what we call in Bologna Pain Special, or special bread. During the Christmas holidays our bakery sold so many of these that we could hardly keep up with demand.

Steps and Procedures

1. In a heavy 3 quart saucepan, heat the honey, sugar, and water cook over low heat until the sugar melts. Remove from the heat and reserve.

2. Soak the raisins in the wine. Sift the flour with the baking powder, cocoa, and salt into a large bowl. Slowly pour in the honey mixture and mix well with a wooden spoon.

3. Stir in the cookie crumbs, jelly, cinnamon, nutmeg, cloves, and vanilla extract. Add the raisins, orange peel, almonds, pine nuts, chocolate, and wine as needed to the mixture and combine.

4. Line two 9-inch cake pans with parchment paper. Grease and reserve. Preheat the oven to 350°F.
5. Pour the batter into the prepared pans. Decorate with candied cherries, candied orange peel, and almonds.
6. Bake in the preheated oven for 45 minutes to 1 hour, or until the cake tests done.
7. Remove cake from the oven and cool before serving.

Decorations
Candied cherries, candied orange peel, toasted almonds

Sfrappole Bolognesi

Fried Sweet Dough

Makes 5 dozen

2¼ cups all-purpose
    flour
⅛ teaspoon salt
½ cup confectioners'
    sugar
4 tablespoons
    unsalted butter,
    melted
1 teaspoon grated
    lemon zest
2 large eggs
2 tablespoons white
    wine or orange
    juice
1 tablespoon milk, as
    needed
Canola oil for deep
    frying
Confectioners' sugar
    to sprinkle on
    after frying

Traditionally prepared for Carnevale these treats are a favorite among young and old. Piled up high on a plate and dusted with powdered sugar they look just like a storybook castle. They can be made in a variety of colors by using food coloring and stored in an airtight container up to 5 days.

Steps and Procedures

1. In the food processor, mix the flour, salt, sugar, butter, lemon zest, and eggs. Slowly add the wine and the milk, using only enough to make the ingredients form a dough.

2. Place the dough on a floured board and knead until smooth and elastic, adding more flour if needed. Dust the dough with flour and roll out into thin strips with the help of a pasta machine (setting 6 on an Imperia machine). Cut into ribbons 2 inches wide.

3. Heat the canola oil in a large, deep frying pan. Test the oil to make sure it is hot enough by dropping in a small piece of dough. Fry 5 or 6 sfrappole at a time until golden brown. Remove them from the oil and drain well on paper towels.

4. Repeat until all the batter is used. Cool and sprinkle the sfrappole with confectioners' sugar before serving.

Ciambella

Sweet Pastry Ring

Serves 8

This is a traditional Bolognese dessert. Every bakery makes a version of it. Some might use the same combination of ingredients but vary the amounts. Or they might substitute olive oil for some of the butter, or sprinkle the pastry with colored sugar. Ciambella can be served for breakfast to dunk in caffè latte, or served as a dessert to dip in wine.

Steps and Procedures

1. Make a ring with the flour, baking powder, sugar, and salt. With the help of a pastry cutter, combine the butter with the flour until it resembles coarse crumbs.
2. In a small bowl, mix together the eggs, milk, vanilla, and lemon zest.
3. Add the egg mixture to the flour and lightly mix the ingredients together until a dough is formed.
4. Preheat the oven to 400°F. Do not over mix or dough will became tough.
5. Turn the dough into a long roll, transfer it to a parchment-lined baking sheet, and close it to form a ring. Make an imprint on the edges with a floured round cookie cutter.
6. Brush the top of ciambella with egg glaze and sprinkle with sugar.
7. Bake for 30 minutes until golden in color. Remove and let it cool before serving.

2 cups all-purpose flour
2 teaspoons baking powder
6 tablespoons unsalted butter, chilled and cut into pieces
½ cup granulated sugar
⅛ teaspoon sea salt
2 large eggs
½ cup whole milk
1 teaspoon vanilla sugar or extract
1 teaspoon lemon zest
Egg wash made by combining 1 egg yolk and 1 tablespoon water
Granulated sugar, for sprinkling

Fishing for Bait

My parents always seemed to me an unusual pair. My mother was so refined, working magic with her hands in the bakery. My father, on the other hand, was a typical outdoorsman. He loved to hunt and fish and tromp around. While time with my mother was magical, time with my father was always filled with fun.

I was the only child in my family for twelve years until my sister Annarita was born. My father deemed it necessary to equip me with skills a father would teach his son. He had a passion for fishing. To this day, when my father comes to the United States he takes a tackle box and rod and heads out toward the stream in my back woods in search of the ideal fishing spot.

My father would prepare for our fishing expeditions by purchasing an oversized bag of bait early in the morning. He would place the tightly sealed bag outside. Once I found the bag and dared my cousin to open it. We carried the bag to the kitchen and proceeded to cut it open and peer inside. Disgusted with the sight of worms, she ran outdoors and I followed laughing, without a thought of closing the bag back up.

A little while later, my mother hurried into the kitchen to finish preparing her food for the trip. As she reached in the sink to remove the drying lettuce for a salad, her hand brushed against something slimy. The bag had tipped over and poured the worms into the sink with all her vegetables. Startled at the sight of so many worms crawling around in her just cleaned food, my mother screamed. My parents never did figure out how the bag got to the kitchen, opened itself, and for fear of being banned from joining them on future fishing trips, I never enlightened them.

Most fishing trips started in a less dramatic fashion—with my parents packing up the car. Over the years we had acquired an entire car full of outdoor gadgets, trying to remember how to assemble them all that made half the fun of the trip. We'd pack all the gadgets into our boat and head out to the water. Emilia Romagna, the region were Bologna is the capital, has two incredible rivers for fishing: the Po River, one of Italy's major rivers, and the Reno River. There are also numerous lakes around Bologna that are ideal for fishing by boat. My family would travel a couple of hours outside of Bologna to find the perfect location on the river edge.

With a spot chosen and the car unpacked, my father would begin the serious task of choosing the right equipment. First he would stare down at the water as if he could see what fish were swimming in the depths below and nod his head as if he were communicating with schools of them. Then he would sit on the ground, his tackle box cradled in his lap, and carefully extract the right lures. I would stand behind him, peering over his shoulder, anxious to begin.

Around this time my mother would call out to him while she was organizing her cooking utensils. She'd ask which fish she should expect, and he'd answer. My father would then fish for hours until he caught not only enough of only that kind of fish, but the healthiest of those.

I would sit with my miniature rod and lure and bob it in and out of the water, hoping a fish had caught and I just didn't notice the tug. But often my rod went empty, while my father's seemed magnetized. Sometimes we'd take my father's boat to a series of small islands just off the coast of Italy and there we'd harvest clams. We'd wait for low tide and watch the sand. Clams will spit water in the air when you walk near them. We'd spot the clams spits and with a long metal rod we'd hook the clams and dig them up.

My mother would always bring a miniature grill to place over the campfire on which she would prepare the fish or clams. She would take the fish and gut them by slicing along the back-bone of the fish to separate the fillets. Then, holding the tail with one hand, she would move her knife along the outside of the fillet to remove the skin in one piece. She had little contain-

Over the years we had acquired an entire car full of outdoor gadgets, trying to remember how to assemble them all that made half the fun of the trip.

ers full of seasonings and herbs and she would season the fillets before she would grill them. She would also prepare various side dishes that she could heat up over the campfire. We'd sit at our table and enjoy an early dinner as the sun started to amble down toward the horizon.

Trota al Pomodoro

Baked Trout with Fresh Tomato and Basil Sauce

Serves 6

Being the daughter of an avid fisherman can have its drawbacks. Not only did we have fish for dinner twice a week; we had a lot of it. The same ones that I had watched swim only a few hours earlier, soon appeared on my dinner plate! As a child, I resented the fact that I was made to eat them. My mother became very good at preparing the fish in many different ways. This recipe using summer tomatoes was my favorite. Today, I only wish I had my father's wonderful fish every time I go to the store to buy some. Make sure to select only the freshest whole fish when cooking it in the oven. Not only will the bones give it a better flavor, they will also keep the fillet moist and juicy. The rule of thumb for cooking fish is to allow 10 minutes for each inch of thickness. The parchment pouches can be prepared several hours ahead and kept in the refrigerator until ready to cook.

Steps and Procedures

1. Prepare the tomatoes by cutting a cross in the bottom squeezing out the seeds, dropping them into boiling water for 3 minutes, then removing and put them in a cold water bath. Peel and chop the tomatoes. In a 2-quart saucepan, add the oil and cook the anchovies, onion, garlic, and capers 2 over high heat for 5 minutes.

2. Add the prepared tomatoes, red pepper, flakes, salt, pepper, and chopped basil and cook oven medium heat for 20 minutes. Prepare the basil butter. Place garlic and basil in the food processor, then process for 2 minutes to mince. Add the softened butter, salt, and pepper, and process to cream. Roll the basil butter in a piece of parchment paper to form a long rope. Refrigerate to set.

12 vine-ripe tomatoes
4 tablespoons olive oil
2 anchovies fillets minced
1 small onion, peeled and minced
2 cloves garlic, peeled and minced
1 teaspoon capers, well rinsed
1/8 teaspoon crushed red pepper flakes
1 teaspoon sea salt
1/2 teaspoon freshly ground black pepper
3 cloves garlic, peeled
1 tablespoon chiffonade fresh basil
6 tablespoons unsalted butter, softened
1 fresh basil leaves, washed and trimmed
3 fresh whole trout, well rinsed
1/2 cup dry white wine

3. Preheat the oven to 400°F. To make parchment pouches begin with three 12-by-18-inch lengths of paper, making sure that they are large enough to hold the trout. Fold the sheets in half to measure 9 by 12 inches. Beginning at the folded edge, draw half a heart shape as large as possible on the paper. Cut it out with scissors. Lightly oil the center of the parchment paper. Place trout in the prepared pouches and place the three pouches on a large baking sheet—do not overcrowd.

4. Sprinkle the inside cavity of each trout with salt, pepper, and wine. Spoon sauce over the trout. Seal each pouch and bake for 20 minutes on a baking sheet. Remove the pouches from the oven. With the help of a spoon, fillet the trout. Once the trout is cooked, the head and bones will come off very easily. Serve with a dollop of prepared basil butter on top.

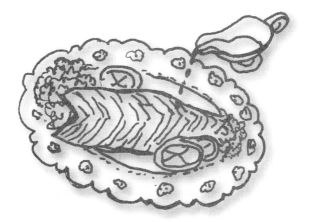

Spaghetti ai Frutti di Mare

Pasta with Seafood Sauce

Serves 6

This is a traditional sauce that is a favorite with seafood lovers. Since the seashore is only a few hours from Bologna, Sundays are perfect for a drive to the beach for some great seafood. I love to make this sauce because it can be prepared quickly and has a great taste. A very important rule when eating a seafood sauce with pasta: Never add cheese. The food would become very difficult to digest, almost like eating a brick.

Steps and Procedures

1. Heat the oil in a 12-inch sauté pan. Add the onions, celery, carrots, garlic, and red pepper flakes. Cook for 5 minutes over medium heat. Add the chopped tomatoes and the wine, and heat through.
2. Add the tomato sauce, parsley, salt, and pepper and simmer for 20 minutes. Add calamari, clams, and mussels, and steam for 5 minutes.
3. Bring a 10-quart pot of water to a boil. Add 1 tablespoon of salt, then the pasta, and cook until al dente. Drain the pasta and toss with the sauce. Serve immediately with a sprinkling of fresh parsley.

¼ cup extra-virgin olive oil

1 onion, peeled and finely minced

1 stalk celery, finely minced

1 carrot, peeled and finely minced

4 cloves garlic, peeled and minced

1 teaspoon crushed red pepper flakes

1 cup tomatoes, peeled, seeded, and chopped

1 tablespoon dry white wine

1 cup tomato sauce

1 teaspoon chopped fresh Italian parsley

1 teaspoon sea salt, see plus 1 additional tablespoon for the pasta cooking water

½ teaspoon freshly ground black pepper

8 ounces calamari, cut into rings

1 pound clams and mussels in their shells

1 pound spaghetti

Chopped fresh parsley for garnish

La Cucina della Mamma

Scampi in Carpione
Marinated Shrimp in Garlic Sauce
Serves 8

¼ cup extra-virgin
  olive oil
1 small onion, peeled
  and minced
1 celery rib, thinly
  sliced
4 cloves garlic, peeled
  and minced
8 ripe Roma
  tomatoes, seeded
  and diced
1 teaspoon sea salt,
  plus additional for
  seasoning shrimp
  to taste
⅛ teaspoon crushed
  red pepper flakes
1 cup freshly squeezed
  orange juice
6 blood oranges,
  peeled, seeded and
  sliced—or substitute
  regular oranges if
  not available
4 tablespoons
  balsamic vinegar
3 pounds shelled and
  deveined scampi or
  large shrimp
¼ cup chopped fresh
  Italian parsley

During the Christmas holidays in the United States you can find blood oranges. They have a terrific flavor and a bright red flesh. In Italy, they are available almost all year long and it's always a treat to freshly squeeze a few or serve them in a salad or dessert. They give an incredible flavor to this recipe. Buy scampi or large white shrimp, shelled and deveined, and do not cook them for more than 4 to 5 minutes.

Steps and Procedures
1. In a 12-inch frying pan, heat the oil and sauté the onion, celery, and garlic until soft. Add the tomatoes, salt, and crushed red pepper. Cook over high heat for 10 minutes. Add the orange juice and reduce over high heat for 10 minutes, stirring once in while.
2. Add the orange slices and balsamic vinegar. Heat and then add shrimp, season with salt, and cook for 5 minutes over medium heat.
3. Sprinkle with parsley and serve.

Insalata di Peperoni

Roasted Pepper Salad

Serves 6

There are three methods for roasting peppers. If you have a gas stove or grill, take the peppers and roast them directly on the open fire, rotating them until the pepper is completely black. Put the peppers in a paper bag, seal, and steam for 10 minutes. Remove the skin, cut off the seeds, and wash them. If using, an electric stove, cut the peppers in half and press them down, put them on a cookie sheet, and put them under the broiler to blacken the skins or roast them in the oven at 400°F. for 23 minutes. Make sure to buy sweet peppers with four or more points at the bottom; they are sweeter than the others. For this recipe use red, yellow, or orange peppers. Remember, green peppers are unripe and very difficult to digest.

Steps and Procedures

1. Prepare a vinaigrette by whisking together the oil, vinegar, garlic, parsley, salt, and pepper.
2. As described above, roast the peppers and remove the skin and seeds. Wash and slice them. Put the peppers onion, and dressing in a large bowl and marinate in the refrigerator for 1 hour, then serve.

½ cup extra-virgin olive oil

¼ cup aged balsamic vinegar

2 cloves garlic, peeled and minced

1 teaspoon chopped fresh Italian parsley

1 teaspoon sea salt

½ teaspoon fresh ground black pepper

6 sweet red, orange, or yellow peppers, roasted and skinned

1 large red onion, peeled and sliced

Perfect Pizza

*D*elicious and tasty, pizza is ideal for a quick snack, a light meal, picnics or at parties. Pizza can change with your moods and taste. Whether you make it with cheese or meat, a thick or thin crust, with seafood or vegetables, hot or cold, pizza is always a hit. A great nutritional alternative to a boring everyday meal, these days we have become so accustomed to having pizza around that we feel as though it's been here forever.

It may be hard to believe, but pizza as we know it is a relatively new creation. In fact, it was introduced by the farmers in Italy, who would enjoy bread as a snack during their long day in the fields. They usually rubbed a red, ripe tomato over the bread followed with a dab of oil and a piece of cheese. As people began to emigrate to this country, they brought their food traditions with them, and one of those traditions was this ancestor of our modern-day pizza.

This simple snack grew rapidly into the pizza we know today. Pizza has become so sophisticated that we sometime feel that we should wear a tux to eat it. In Italy, pizza is served in single portions. It will have very little sauce but lots of cheese and is usually baked in a brick oven. It's also considered rude in Italy to eat pizza with your hands. Let your imaginations go wild. Pizza will always taste great.

Making pizza can be very easy if you follow these steps:

1. Always preheat your oven to 400°F.
2. Use a pizza stone or an extra cookie sheet on which to bake the pizza.
3. Remember to keep yeast proofing in a warm spot.
4. Make sure your yeast is fresh.
5. Use bread flour high in protein so gluten will develop.
6. Pizza can be prepared in a variety of ways, white or with sauce, thick or thin, stuffed or plain.

Pizzette

Little White Pizza with Arugula and Artichoke Hearts

Serves 12

This is my mother's special pizza dough recipe. It is easy to prepare and can be placed in the freezer for up to 3 months. Use fresh yeast only if you can buy it directly from a bakery; most supermarket yeast is already past its prime. The starter can be kept in the refrigerator in a sealed container for 2 days.

1 cup warm water (95° to 110°F.)

1 teaspoon dry yeast

1 teaspoon granulated sugar

3 cups bread flour

1 tablespoons dry milk

½ cup shortening

2 tablespoons extra-virgin olive oil

1 teaspoon salt

1 tablespoon cornmeal

2 cups, chopped marinated artichokes hearts, reserving marinade

1 cup shredded fresh arugula

1 pound fresh mozzarella cheese, sliced

Steps and Procedures

1. Place the water in a bowl; stir in the yeast and sugar. Cover with a wet cloth and let it proof for 10 minutes in a warm spot.
2. Make a starter by mixing 1 cup of the flour with the proofed yeast. Add the milk, shortening, and oil. Mix well with the help of a fork. The dough will be sticky and wet. Put it in a bowl covered with a wet cloth and allow to rest for 30 or more minutes in a warm spot away from drafts.
3. Add the remaining 2 cups of flour and the salt. Mix the ingredients well. Work the dough with the heel of your hands until smooth and elastic. (Add flour or water if needed.) Make the dough into a ball and place it in an oiled bowl. Cover with a wet cloth. Let the dough rise until double in bulk (about 20 minutes).
4. Punch the dough down and divide it into twelve pieces. Shape them into round balls. Roll each out to a 4-inch circle. Line 2 large cookie sheets with parchment paper and sprinkle with cornmeal. Allow the dough to rise. Preheat the oven to 400°F.
5. Brush the pizzas with the marinade from the artichokes. Top each with artichokes, arugula, and mozzarella prior to baking. Bake for 10 to 15 minutes, until cheese bubbles and melts. Remove from the oven and serve.

Torta Salata

Savory Tart

Serves 8

Tart Dough
2 cups all-purpose
   flour
1 teaspoon sea salt
8 teaspoons unsalted
   butter, chilled
2 egg yolks
5 tablespoons ice
   water

Filling
2 tablespoons extra-
   virgin olive oil
1 small onion, peeled
   and finely chopped
2 cloves garlic, peeled
   and minced
2 pounds baby
   portobello
   mushrooms,
   cleaned and sliced
¼ cup dried porcini
   mushrooms,
   soaked in water,
   then drained,
   reserving the
   liquid

Perfect for a picnic or a light supper, vegetable tarts can be made ahead with a variety of fillings. Take into consideration seasonal vegetables: zucchini, squashes, asparagus, peppers, and onions all work well in tarts. Have all the ingredients for making the dough chilled, and work the dough as little as possible so as to develop the gluten in the flour. Prepare ahead and freeze. Before serving, bring tart to room temperature then bake at 350°F. for 20 minutes.

Steps and Procedures
1. To make the tart, preheat the oven to 400°F. Sift the flour onto a work surface and make a well in the center. Add the salt, and with a wide-hole grater, grate the butter into the center. Work with your fingertips to incorporate the butter with the flour until it resembles course crumbs. Whisk the egg yolks with the water and add the mixture to the well. Gradually draw from the flour, pushing the dough onto the cutting board to knead. If the dough feels too dry, sprinkle with a few drops of water.
2. Gather the dough in a rough ball and with the heel of your hand push the sections of the dough down and away from you, smearing the flour and butter together against the work surface. Gather the dough and repeat once more. Shape dough into a flat ball, wrap, and chill for 30 minutes. (The first step can also be done in a food processor: put the flour, salt and cold butter, cut in tiny pieces, in the work bowl fitted with a steel blade. Process on/off until you have achieved a pea like texture. Add the eggs and pour the water through the feed tube while processing in

quick bursts until the dough forms a mass. Gather, wrap, and chill.)

3. To make the filling, in a 12-inch frying pan, heat the oil, then add the onions, garlic, portobellos, and drained porcini mushrooms, and sauté over high heat for 10 minutes, until they began to soften. Deglaze with brandy and the strained porcini water. Cook for 20 minutes over low heat. Add 1 teaspoon of the salt, the black pepper and the parsley. Remove and cool.

4. In a small bowl, whisk the eggs with the cream. Season with the remaining salt, plus the pepper and nutmeg, and stir the custard into the cooled mushroom mixture.

5. Roll out the chilled dough on a floured marble cutting board ¼ inch thick. Put the dough in a buttered 9-inch tart pan with a removable bottom. Push the dough down to make it fit the pan. Do not stretch the dough or it will shrink. Use the rolling pin to roll over. With the help of a rolling pin or a knife, cut off excess dough from sides of the tart pan. With a fork, mark the dough at the bottom of the pan. Cover with plastic wrap and chill in the refrigerator for 30 minutes.

6. Pour the mushroom mixture into the prepared tart shell. Bake in the preheated oven for about 35 or 40 minutes, or until it is golden brown on top.

7. Set it cool completely, then cut into wedges and serve.

¼ cup brandy
2 teaspoons sea salt
1 teaspoon freshly ground black pepper
1 teaspoon chopped fresh Italian parsley
2 large eggs
1 cup heavy whipping cream
½ teaspoon freshly ground white pepper
⅛ teaspoon freshly grated nutmeg

Zuppa Imperiale

Imperial Soup

Serves 8

6 eggs, separated
8 tablespoons
    semolina flour
8 tablespoons freshly
    grated
    Parmigiano
    Reggiano cheese
6 tablespoons butter,
    melted and cooled
1 teaspoon sea salt
½ teaspoon freshly
    ground black
    pepper
½ teaspoon freshly
    grated nutmeg
2 quarts defatted
    broth, heated

Here's an elegant soup served only on special occasions. The secret for good soup is in the broth. A good broth, made from capon or beef, or consommé is a must for this recipe. Prepare the dough ahead of time, it will keep for several days. To give more flavor to the dough, add finely minced prosciutto or mortadella or some fresh herbs. Cut the cubes into a uniform ½-inch size.

Steps and Procedures
1. Preheat the oven to 350°F. Butter and line a 9-by-12-inch baking pan with parchment paper.
2. In a bowl, beat the egg yolks, then slowly add the semolina flour and grated cheese. Add butter and continue beating while adding salt, pepper, and nutmeg.
3. Beat the egg whites with a pinch of salt until stiff. Fold it into the egg-yolk mixture and pour batter into prepared pan.
4. Put pan in the oven. Bake for about 20 to 25 minutes until lightly browned. Cool.
5. Cut the bread into small cubes. Divide the cubes among eight soup bowls. Pour the hot broth over the cubes and serve.

Arrista di Maiale alla Panna

Loin of Pork in Creamy Sauce

Serves 8

This is one of my mother's specialties. She would prepare it on Sundays and serve it with oven-roasted potatoes and seasonal vegetables infused with lemon citronette. A real treat for all the senses. This very delicate dish can be prepared ahead of time.

Steps and Procedures

1. Put the herb rub ingredients in the food processor and process until minced. Set aside.
2. In a large 12-inch frying pan, melt butter and olive oil. Cook the onion and garlic for 5 minutes over high heat. Preheat the oven to 350°F.
3. Massage the pork with herb rub, top with thyme and rosemary sprigs, and wrap with butcher string.
4. Add the prepared pork roast to the pan and brown well on both sides. Sprinkle with wine and let it evaporate.
5. Transfer the pork roast to a 13-by-9-inch baking dish and add the stock, bay leaves, and the cream.
6. Cover with foil and bake for 55 minutes, or until an instant-read thermometer reads 170°F.
7. Remove the pan from the oven. Strain the sauce and adjust the seasoning with salt and pepper as needed. Cool the roast, then remove the strings and the fresh herb sprigs.
8. Slice and put the pork on a serving dish. Pour the sauce over the meat, then serve.

Herb Rub

1 teaspoon fresh rosemary
1 teaspoon fresh sage
½ teaspoon fresh thyme
4 cloves garlic, peeled
1 teaspoon coarse sea salt

6 tablespoons unsalted butter
2 tablespoon extra-virgin olive oil
1 small onion, peeled and chopped
3 garlic cloves, peeled and minced
3 pounds center-cut boneless pork loin, trimmed
2 to 3 sprigs fresh rosemary
2 to 3 fresh thyme sprigs
½ cup dry white wine
½ cup beef stock
2 bay leaves
2 cups heavy whipping cream
½ teaspoon sea salt
1 teaspoon freshly ground white pepper

La Cucina della Mamma

163

Tacchino della Mamma

Turkey Breast with Fontina Cheese and Porcini Sauce

Serves 8

2 tablespoons extra-
  virgin olive oil
4 ounces dried porcini
  mushrooms,
  soaked, then
  drained
1 cup sliced cremini
  mushrooms
4 cloves garlic,
  minced
8 slices boneless and
  skinless turkey
  breast
½ cup dry white wine
½ cup chicken stock
1 teaspoon marjoram
½ teaspoon thyme
1 teaspoon sea salt
1 teaspoon freshly
  ground white
  pepper
⅛ teaspoon freshly
  grated nutmeg
¼ cup grated
  Parmigiano
  Reggiano cheese
1 pound sliced fontina
  cheese
2 cups béchamel sauce
  (see page 44)

Here's a traditional Bolognese dish created at the restaurant Don Chisciotte, owned by Cavaliere Lambertini, who was also the owner of the bakery La Canasta, where my mother was the head pastry chef until she opened her own bakery.

Steps and Procedures
1. Heat the oil in a deep sauté pan. Add the chopped porcini and cremini, mushrooms, and the garlic.
2. Add the turkey slices and lightly brown each on both sides. Add the wine and cook until it evaporates. Sprinkle with marjoram and thyme. Remove the turkey and reserve in a baking dish. Preheat the oven to 350°F.
3. Add the béchamel sauce to the mushroom mixture.
4. Add the Parmigiano Reggiano cheese. Season with nutmeg, salt, and pepper.
5. Place the fontina slices on top of the turkey. Pour sauce over the prepared turkey slices. Cover with foil.
6. Bake for 30 minutes in the preheated oven, then serve.

Fettine di Vitello alla Petroniana

Veal Scaloppine with Prosciutto

Serves 8

A traditional Bolognese specialty, it is made in many different ways, rolled up or flat. My mother made them rolled up and she would grate some fresh truffles on top.

Steps and Procedures

1. Melt the butter in a skillet and sauté the onion and the celery until the onion is transparent. Remove from heat. In a bowl, combine the onion mixture, bread crumbs, eggs, thyme, parsley, nutmeg, cheese, salt, and pepper. Pound the scaloppine between sheets of plastic wrap with a flat meat mallet. Season with salt and pepper.

2. Place each scaloppine on top of a slice of prosciutto. Spread ¼ cup of the stuffing mixture on each scaloppine. Roll each up so the prosciutto is on the outside and the filling inside, then secure with 2 toothpicks.

2 tablespoons
   unsalted butter
1 onion, finely
   chopped
½ cup celery, finely
   chopped
2 cups fresh bread
   crumbs
2 large eggs
1 teaspoon thyme
½ cup chopped fresh
   Italian parsley
⅛ teaspoon grated
   nutmeg
½ cup grated
   Parmigiano
   Reggiano cheese
1 teaspoon sea salt, plus
   additional to taste
½ teaspoon freshly
   ground black
   pepper, plus
   additional to taste
8 veal scaloppine cut
   from the top round
   of the leg

(Continued)

¼ pound prosciutto, thinly sliced into 8 portions
Olive oil for frying, 6 tablespoons
1 cup cleaned and sliced mushrooms
2 cloves garlic, minced
1 cup dry white wine
1 cup defatted chicken stock
1 tablespoon tomato paste

3. Sauté the veal in oil in a 12-inch skillet until lightly browned. Add the mushrooms and garlic and cook until soft. Season to taste with salt and pepper. Add the white wine and reduce the liquid for 5 minutes over high heat.

4. Add the stock and tomato paste and cook for 20 minutes at a simmer. Season to taste with salt and pepper.

5. Serve the scaloppine with the reduced wine sauce.

Torta di Mandorle di Frutta

Almond Torte with Fresh Fruit

Serves 8

Use a variety of fresh fruits when making this delicious almond torte. My mother made it at her bakery on a large sheet tray and sold it by weight. This torte can be made ahead and frozen before being garnished with fresh fruit and brushed with apricot glaze.

Steps and Procedures

1. Preheat the oven to 375°F. Butter the bottom of a 9-inch cake pan. Line the bottom of the cake pan with parchment and then more butter.
2. In a food processor, chop the almonds with the sugar until very fine. Sift together the flour, baking powder, and salt.
3. Cream the butter in an electric mixer until light and fluffy. Add the almond and vanilla extracts and the lemon zest. Beat until thoroughly incorporated. Add the eggs, one at a time, beating continuously.
4. Fold in the nuts and flour mixture.
5. Pour the batter into the prepared pan and bake on the center rack for 35 minutes. Remove the pan from the oven to cool. Remove the cake from its pan and set it on a cake rack, discard the paper, and cool completely. Chill for 30 minutes.
6. To make the glaze, heat the jelly with the liqueur in the top of a double boiler for 20 minutes. Strain the mixture through a fine sieve.
7. Decorate the cake with slices of fresh fruit, then brush the fruit with the prepared glaze. Cool before serving.

Melted butter for preparing the cake pan
1 cup blanched whole almonds
⅔ cup granulated sugar
1 cup all-purpose flour
1 teaspoon baking powder
½ teaspoon salt
8 tablespoons unsalted butter, softened
2 drops almond extract
1 teaspoon vanilla extract
1 teaspoon grated lemon zest
3 large eggs
Fresh fruits: peaches, strawberries, raspberries, and blackberries

Apricot Glaze
½ cup apricot jelly
1 tablespoon Amaretto liqueur

La Cucina della Mamma

Making Risotto

I've always wondered about taste buds—how one food is loved and another rejected; how some food can be disliked at first and slowly grow to become a favorite. What makes a flavor so wonderfully appealing that it becomes a lifelong memory of your mother's cooking? Every child has a favorite dish that was made by a parent. It is a taste or smell that reminds you of the warmth and security of your parents' home. Often favorite dishes are comfort food rich in calories and flavor. But what is it about the dish that makes it such a unique gastronomic treat?

I could smell my favorite dish cooking before I had reached the door to our home after school. The soaking mushrooms sent a cloud of aroma through the house and under the front door to greet my nose as I turned the street corner. A smile would spread across my face, as I'd run the rest of the way home. That smell meant my mother was home early from work and that she was making my favorite dish, *Risotto con i Funghi*.

Risotto is a time-rich dish. Rumored to have been around since the fifteenth century, risotto is not cooked but created. It begins slowly, the rice pores must be tempted open with butter, and only a little stock added at a time to allow the hungry rice to absorb the rich drink. All the while, the rice must be slowly stirred, always in the same direction, always with the same rhythm and strength. My mother was very protective of her risotto. Only my mother could stir the rice since she firmly believed even a slight variation in the rhythm lessened the greatness of the dish. I would push a kitchen stool next to the stove and watch the rice slowly come alive and turn the milky rich consistency of risotto. While I supervised the evolution of the dish, my mother would ask about my day. Some mothers share stories over a glass of milk and cookies, my mother used risotto. I felt privileged to be permitted to witness the creation of that dish since my father was banned from the kitchen years before for attempting to add too much cheese to the rice. I alone was allowed to spend the afternoon making risotto with Mamma.

Risotto waits for no one. The rice reaches the perfect consistency and temperature for only a few moments. It is during that window of opportunity that the dish should be served and eaten to savor the burst of flavor of the risotto. It was a bittersweet moment for me when the dish reached perfection. It meant soon my time alone with my mother would end, but it also meant we'd be feasting on the succulent mixture. Mamma would warn me, "Okay, Loretta, time to get ready," and I'd race around the kitchen gathering the wide bowls used for serving the risotto.

Even with the creation of so many great "quick-and-easy" recipes, risotto is still worth the extra time. However, I have learned later in life, that risotto, even if not made with such care, can still hold as much wonderful flavor as it did back then. Nowadays, when I smell the pungent aroma of porcini mushrooms being slowly swirled into a pot of risotto, it isn't the flavor of that dish that I instantly recall, but the image of my mother slowly stirring the rice, listening attentively to my day's adventures. I wonder if the taste buds are more directly linked to the heart than to the stomach.

Risotto waits

for no one.

Risotto

In Italy, risotto is not just another rice dish; it is a passion.

Ask any Italian, and he will tell you that the secret to making a good risotto is pazienza *(patience). You see, it takes 20 minutes for the risotto to cook.*

Time is not the only factor in making a good risotto. You also need the right equipment, rice, and broth.

The equipment is simple. You'll need a heavy pan with a copper bottom for even distribution of heat, a wooden spoon for gently stirring the rice, and, of course, a strong arm!

Choosing the rice and broth to make a risotto is simple, too. You need superfino rice, good-quality rice that is plump, hardy, and full of starch. Arborio rice is best because it withstands the long cooking process and still keeps a bite al dente. *Also, it has enough starch to give* risotto al'onda *the wavy look. The broth is what gives the risotto its flavor. Use good clear chicken, meat, or fish broth.*

The proportions for risotto are 1 cup dry rice to 2½ cups liquid. (This makes enough for two people.) Cooking risotto is a ritual. Begin by melting a little butter and olive oil in a heavy-bottomed pan. Add a soffritto, *a mixture of finely minced onion, celery, and carrots. Stir in the rice and cook for 2 to 3 minutes. Add the white wine and let it evaporate so the steam will start to cook the rice and the starch can be released. Slowly add the hot broth. Reduce the heat to a simmer and gently stir the mixture with a wooden spoon. After 23 minutes, the rice grains will begin to stick together. Sprinkle a little grated Parmigiano cheese over it, add 1 tablespoon butter, and serve. The Italians call this final step* montecare, *the mounting of the risotto.*

Close your eyes when you take your first bite of risotto and you will know what all the fuss is about.

Risotto al Pomodoro

Risotto with Fresh Tomato and Basil Sauce

Serves 6

This is a very simple recipe that requires a little patience and a lot of stirring. The wonderful flavor comes from the oven-roasted tomatoes; do not substitute dried or canned tomatoes. I make tomato roses by removing the skin from the tomatoes with a pairing knife or a vegetable peeler in one long strip, then rolling it up and making it sit on its base. Place one tomato rose on each plate with two basil leaves on each side. Use the pulp after the seeds have been removed, cut into small dice, to sprinkle it on top of the risotto before serving. There is nothing that compares to the flavor of freshly cooked risotto. Create a wonderful dinner party by having every ingredients ready mise en place and have your guest take turns stirring. Unfortunately, many restaurants in the United States precook their risotto and chill it. When it is ordered, they warm it up and finish it with cream to give it texture.

Steps and Procedures

1. Preheat the oven to 400°F. Put the tomato halves skin-side down on a cookie sheet lined with parchment paper. Sprinkle with salt and olive oil and roast for 20 minutes. Remove from the oven and let the tomatoes cool. Next skin them and chop.
2. Heat the stock in a 2-quart saucepan. Melt 4 tablespoons of the butter in a 6-quart saucepan. Add the garlic, onion, and basil and cook over high heat for 5 minutes.
3. Lower the heat and add the rice, tossing while stirring for 2 minutes.
4. Add wine and cook over high heat for 5 minutes.
5. Add the roasted tomatoes, tomato paste, salt, and pepper, and cook for an additional 5 minutes over high heat.

2 pounds ripe Roma tomatoes, cut in half and seeded
1 teaspoon sea salt, plus additional to taste
Olive oil
4 cups chicken stock
6 tablespoons unsalted butter
4 cloves garlic, peeled and minced
1 small onion, peeled and finely minced
2 tablespoons shredded fresh basil, plus additional for garnish
2 cups raw Arborio, Carnaroli, or Vialone Nano rice
½ cup dry white wine
1 teaspoon tomato paste
½ cup freshly grated Parmigiano Reggiano

La Cucina della Mamma

6. Lower the heat to a simmer and stir in the heated stock a little at a time. Keep stirring and adding broth for 23 minutes at a simmer.

7. *Mantecare* by stirring in the remaining butter and continue stirring until all the liquid is absorbed. Risotto should be al dente.

8. Season with salt and pepper to taste. Sprinkle with basil and Parmigiano Reggiano cheese and serve.

Risotto alla Rucola

Risotto with Arugula and Gorgonzola Cheese

Serves 8

This dish is very appealing to all the senses and will bring many compliments at your dinner parties. You will find it perfect for a light spring supper served with a tossed salad and fresh strawberries with balsamic vinegar for dessert.

Steps and Procedures

1. Heat the oil in large 12-inch sauté pan. Cook the shallot over high heat until soft.
2. Add the rice, stir, and cook for 2 minutes. Add the wine and lower the heat to a simmer, then stir until the wine has evaporated.
3. Slowly add hot stock a little at the time. Stir continuously and add salt and pepper to taste. Continue cooking over low heat while adding more hot broth as needed. Make sure that the rice is covered with liquid at all times.
4. Approximately 5 minutes before the rice is ready, stop adding the broth and allow the rice to absorb the remaining liquid. Taste and adjust seasoning.
5. The rice will be done in approximately 23 minutes. Add the arugula, lemon juice, and zest.
6. To *montecare* the risotto, stir in the butter and Gorgonzola cheese at the very end of the cooking time.
7. When rice is al dente, transfer it to a serving dish. Sprinkle with parsley and cheese before serving.

2 tablespoons extra-virgin olive oil
1 shallot, peeled and minced
2 cups Arborio rice
¼ cup dry white wine
4½ cups chicken stock
1 teaspoon sea salt
½ teaspoon lemon pepper
1 cup fresh arugula, washed, trimmed, and shredded
4 tablespoons fresh lemon juice
1 teaspoon grated lemon zest
2 tablespoons unsalted butter
¼ pound Gorgonzola cheese, crumbled
1 teaspoon chopped fresh Italian parsley
1 tablespoon freshly grated Parmigiano Reggiano cheese

Agnello al Rosmarino

Lamb Stew with Rosemary Potatoes and Olives

Serves 8

2 pounds boneless
lamb stew meat,
from the loin or leg,
trimmed and cut up
1/4 cup dry white wine
1/2 teaspoon fresh
thyme leaves
1 teaspoon chopped
fresh rosemary
1 teaspoon sea salt,
plus additional to
taste
1 teaspoon freshly
ground white
pepper, plus
additional to taste
4 tablespoons extra-
virgin olive oil
2 anchovy fillets, minced
1 tablespoon capers,
rinsed well
2 all-purpose
potatoes, peeled
and quartered
1 small onion, peeled
and chopped
4 cloves garlic, peeled
and minced
1 cup chicken stock
2 teaspoons chopped
fresh Italian parsley
1/4 cup lemon juice
1/2 cup pitted black
olives

Lamb is traditionally served during Easter season. This stew is flavored with fresh rosemary and olives, combined with potatoes. Buy young spring lamb, no older than 6 months. The older the animal, the stronger the flavor. By government standards only after one year of age is lamb considered mutton. Do not overcook the lamb or it will become tough.

Steps and Procedures:

1. Marinate the lamb in wine, thyme, and 1/2 teaspoon of the rosemary. Season with salt and pepper and put the bowl in the refrigerator for 2 hours.

2. In a 6-quart casserole, heat the oil and over high heat cook the anchovies, capers, potatoes, onion, and garlic until soft. Add the lamb, reserving the marinade. Brown the meat while stirring on all sides.

3. Add the marinade and cook to evaporate. Add the broth and cook at a simmer for 30 minutes.

4. Season the stew with parsley, salt, and pepper. Add the lemon juice. Simmer until the lamb and potatoes are tender—another 10 minutes. Add the olives and reduce the liquid.

5. Serve the stew with a sprinkle of fresh chopped rosemary.

Bollito con Salsa Verde

Steamed Fillet with Caper and Parsley Sauce

Serves 8

Once a week my mother would make broth that would be used for the week. She would buy a piece of lesso, the Italian version of beef brisket, an inexpensive cut of beef, plus bones from the butcher for the stock. After cooking them for a few hours, she had a great broth and a piece of meat for that evening's supper. Since the flavor of that tender piece of meat was somewhat bland, she would serve it with salsa verde, a spicy sauce. The stock may be reduced by half and frozen in ice cube trays, then bagged for quick sauce making or pan deglazing. Stock may be reduced further for an intense meat glaze. Bones and parts for the stock can be purchased over the counter in large supermarkets. Veal bones add body to the stock—don't omit them.

Steps and Procedures

1. To make the stock, put the meat and bones in a large 10-quart stockpot, add cold water, and bring to a rapid boil. Skim the scum as it rises to the surface. Turn the heat low, add the vegetables and seasonings and simmer the stock very gently for three to four hours, skimming occasionally. Remove the meat from the broth and reserve it. Cool the stock for 30 minutes in a sink filled with ice water.

2. Strain the stock through a sieve. Refrigerate overnight for easy removal of fat from the surface. Transfer the defatted stock to a container and refrigerate for 1 week or freeze for up to 2 months.

3. To make the herb sauce, in the food processor mix together

Brodo di Carne (Beef Stock)

2 to 3 pounds boneless beef chuck eye roast or fresh beef brisket

1 pound chicken feet, backs, and necks

1 pound veal knuckle bones

4 quarts cold water

1 carrot, chopped

1 large onion, peeled and chopped

1 celery rib, with leaves chopped

1 tomato

1 garlic clove

4 to 5 parsley sprigs

8 black peppercorns

See page 176 for *Salsa Verde* Ingredients

Salsa Verde (Herb Sauce)

¼ *cup white wine*
   vinegar
1 cup chopped fresh
   Italian parsley
1 hard-boiled egg
2 anchovy fillets
1 tablespoon capers,
   rinsed well
½ *teaspoon sea salt*
½ *cup extra-virgin*
   olive oil

the vinegar, parsley, egg, anchovies, capers, and salt. With the machine running add the oil. Adjust seasoning and reserve.

4. To complete the dish, slice the beef and arrange it on a serving dish, spoon *salsa verde* on top, and serve.

Crocchette di Semolino

Semolina Dumplings

Serves 8

These little morsels make a great appetizer. Make them ahead, freeze them, and cook them right before serving. During Mardi Gras they are made in a sweet version by adding sugar to the semolina flour and sprinkling with confectioners' sugar after they are fried.

Steps and Procedures

1. Heat the milk in a 1-quart saucepan. Melt the butter in a 2-quart saucepan set over low heat. Slowly whisk the semolina flour into the butter and stir until a smooth paste is achieved. Slowly add the heated milk and stir until smooth.

2. Cook over low heat for about 10 minutes, stirring constantly. Season with salt, pepper, and nutmeg, and remove the pan from the heat. Add the grated cheese and stir to incorporate.

3. Cool the mixture slightly; cover with plastic wrap, taking care that a crust doesn't form on the top.

4. Add 2 of the eggs one at a time, stirring well after each addition. With a wet spatula, spread the mixture evenly onto well-buttered cookie sheets.

5. Let the mixture cool; cover with plastic wrap and chill for about 2 hours in the refrigerator. With a wet knife, cut into the dough into 16 to 20 equal pieces.

6. Form the pieces into croquettes. Beat the remaining eggs with the milk. Roll each croquette in flour, dip into the egg mixture, and cover completely with more flour. Fry in oil (making sure that the oil is not too hot or they will split) until golden brown, or bake in a preheated 400°F. oven for 25 minutes. Drain on paper towels and serve.

1½ cups whole milk
8 tablespoons
    unsalted butter
8 tablespoons
    semolina flour
1 teaspoon sea salt
½ teaspoon freshly
    ground white
    pepper
⅛ teaspoon grated
    nutmeg
1 cup freshly grated
    Parmigiano
    Reggiano cheese
4 large eggs
1 teaspoon whole milk
2 cups all-purpose
    flour
2 cups canola or
    vegetable oil for
    frying

Gnocchi di Crema

Fried Sweet Cream

Serves 8

2 cups whole milk,
   plus 1 additional
   teaspoon
¼ cup granulated
   sugar
⅛ teaspoon sea salt
½ cup all-purpose
   flour
5 large whole eggs
2 cups plain fresh
   bread crumbs
2 cups canola or
   vegetable oil for
   frying
1 cup granulated
   sugar for garnish
1 teaspoon vanilla
   sugar
1 teaspoon lemon zest

You can't eat just one of these little morsels. They are traditional part of the fritto misto **Bolognese,** *a delightful array of meats, fruits, and vegetables lightly coated and fried. A favorite restaurant of our family in Bologna was Da Guido, and this was one of the many specialties. When my future father-in-law came to meet my family, we took him there for dinner. He ordered the* fritto misto *and loved the* gnocchi di crema *but was reluctant to try the fried brains, especially since he was a psychiatrist.*

Steps and Procedures

1. In a two-quart saucepan heat 2 cups of the milk but do not boil. Whisk 3 of the eggs with the sugar, vanilla sugar, lemon zest, salt, and flour. Temper the milk with the eggs. Slowly add the rest of the milk, constantly whisking with a wooden spoon. Allow the cream to cook over low heat for 10 minutes, or until it coats the back of a spoon. Butter a cookie sheet.
2. Pour hot cream on to the prepared cookie sheet. Spread the mixture with a flat spatula to a 1 inch thickness. Cover with plastic wrap and refrigerate for 2 hours to cool.
3. When the cream has completely cooled, cut it with a wet knife into diamond shapes. In a small bowl beat the remaining eggs with the milk.
4. Dredge gnocchi in bread crumbs, then dip into the beaten eggs, and back into the bread crumbs.
5. Fry the gnocchi in very hot oil until lightly browned. Drain on paper towels. Roll the gnocchi in sugar and serve.

Mistocchine

Sweet Rolls

Makes 12

Chestnut trees line the streets of Bologna. During the fall, vendors will be at every corner selling hot little bundles of steaming roasted chestnuts. My mother would use chestnuts in several preparations in the bakery. She would coat some in sugar syrup for marron Glacé and make chestnut rolls that she would fill with whipped cream and serve with hot chocolate or cappuccino.

1 teaspoon dry yeast
½ cup warm water
½ cup granulated sugar
½ cup unsalted butter melted, cooled, plus extra for brushing on rolls
½ teaspoon anise extract
½ teaspoon ground cinnamon
½ teaspoon freshly grated nutmeg
1½ teaspoons freshly grated orange zest
½ cup chestnut flour
1½ cups bread flour
¼ teaspoon sea salt

Steps and Procedures:

1. Proof the yeast in warm water until it bubbles. Combine it with the sugar. In a large mixing bowl, stir in the butter, anise, cinnamon, nutmeg, and zest.

2. Sift the flours and salt, and mix into the butter mixture. Mix in the proofed yeast. Put the dough on a floured board and knead until smooth and elastic, adding more flour or water as needed.

3. Transfer the dough to an oiled bowl. Cover the bowl with a dishtowel and let it rest until it doubles in bulk at least 1 hour.

4. Punch dough down and divide it into 12 equal pieces. Roll each one into a round ball. Place them all on a parchment paper–lined cookie sheet. Preheat the oven to 350°F.

5. Brush the rolls with melted butter. Let the rolls rise for 20 minutes, then bake for 20 minutes, or until golden in color.

6. Cool the rolls in the pan for 15 minutes. Serve with coffee or hot chocolate.

Bibliography

E. Calzolan, A. Moeisi, S. Nanetti, L. Beletti. *Diventare Cuoco*. Bologna: Calderoni, 1985.

Liliana Babbi Cappelletti. *Civiltà della Tavola Contadina in Romagna*. Milan: Idealibri, Prima Edizione, 1993.

Ricette di Osterie. *Dell' Emilia dall' Uovo al Maiale*. Milan: Slow Food Edition, 1997.

Fernanda Gosetti. *Il Dolcissimo*. Milan: Gruppo Editoriale Fabbri, Bompian, Souzoguo, Etas s.p.a. Prima Edizione, 1984.

Fernanda Gosetti. *In Cucina con Fernanda Gosetti*. Milan: Gruppa Souzoguo, 1978.

Nika Hazelton. *The Regional Italian Kitchen*. New York: M. Evans and Company, 1978.

Paolo Petroui. *Il Libro della Vera Cucina Emiliana*. Florence: Casa Editrice Bonechi, 1992.

Renzo Portalupi. *Il Grande Libro dei Prima Piatti*. Milan: Mariotti Publishing, 1994.

Giovanna Salvodi: *La Cucina Emiliana e Romagnola. Le Tradizioni a Tavola*. Florence: Edizioni del Riccio, 1987.

Monica Cesari Sartoni and Alessandro Molinari Pradelli. *La Cucina Bolognese*. Rome: Newton & Compton, 1996.

Index